Table of Content

I0011456

Preface

Introduction

Search is everywhere, yet it is one of the most misunderstood functionalities of the IT industry. It is an incredibly useful feature that most people (including developers) take for granted, unless it's missing or poorly implemented—and then you frustrate and annoy your users.

Enterprise search never used to be for the faint of heart, or for those who possessed a thin wallet; it frequently needed a lot of time and deep pockets to get it right. Apache Solr has changed all that.

Figure 1: Apache Solr Logo

Even though Apache Solr is highly popular, getting started can sometimes be daunting. That's what motivated me to write this book. While there's a lot of information about search engines and Solr, in my opinion, it's not simple enough to get some people started—information is scattered all over the place and often difficult to find. The Solr Wiki is very complete, but deeply technical, and in many cases, scares beginners away.

Of course you also have the option to evaluate other commercial search engines, but they can be hugely expensive and require a steep learning curve. Because of this, Solr has rapidly become the number one choice. This is my personal opinion, but it is shared by thousands of developers and companies all over the world.

Most importantly however, I have a promise for you.

My Promise to You

I promise that in the next couple of hours and hundred pages, I will teach you to build something that might take you weeks to learn on your own. Together we'll create a search experience that, if done from scratch, could cost thousands of dollars to build, and we'll have a lot of fun along the way. That's not bad for a free e-book right? However, here's my disclaimer: it's not going to be a fully advanced and complete application, and I will be leaving lots of room for improvement and expansion. I will promise you though, that it will be an amazing start and a very interesting journey.

Who is This Book For?

This book is for developers in the software industry who are looking for a gentle introduction to creating enterprise-scale search solutions. It's for the project managers whose technical teams are telling them, "We desperately need a search solution in our project." It's for the bosses and the administrators who've never had to build or maintain a search solution before.

It's not for those of you who already know what Apache Solr is and how it works, and it's most definitely not for those who are looking for tech-heavy articles on digging into the source code, or optimizing their installations.

If you're an enterprise search newcomer looking for a gentle introduction, then this book is for you!

This is *Apache Solr Succinctly*.

Code Examples

All code examples in this book can be found on GitHub at
https://github.com/xaviermorera/solr-succinctly.git.

Acknowledgements

Special thanks to Syncfusion for providing me with the opportunity to author this book, to Pluralsight for the support on the creation of **Getting Started with Enterprise Search using Apache Solr** training, and to Search Technologies for initiating me into the wonderful world of search engines.

And of course, to my wife for being so patient with me on all my endeavors, which includes a lot of up to 16-hour workdays and 80-hour workweeks. And to my reasons for living, my daughters Juli and Luci.

Chapter 1 Why Solr and Enterprise Search?

Search is Everywhere

Internet search, mainly because of Google, has an interesting side effect: people expect search everywhere.

There are billions of people trained in search on a global scale, something you simply couldn't afford to pay the training costs for. Yet, Google by its very way of doing business did just this—and mostly for zero cost, ensuring billions of daily searches as of 2013, and growing.

Where do we see search applications? You have YAHOO! for web search, a search box in the top right for your files in Windows Explorer, Spotlight in Mac, the Charms bar in Windows 8, Bing, Outlook, iPhone, and Android; the list is huge and seemingly never-ending.

Search is everywhere to make your life easy in all aspects.

Figure 2: Various Search Tools

There is far more to search than meets the eye, however. Mr. Kamran Khan, CEO of Search Technologies, says that in the majority of cases there are only two types of search: outside the firewall, and inside the firewall. Outside the firewall is used to make money, and inside the firewall to save money.

So I asked, "why?"

- Outside the firewall search is a powerful tool for selling. Think, for example, of eBay and Amazon. A good search in an e-commerce site allows a customer to find what he or she is looking for and purchase. Ka-ching! The cash register is happy!
- Inside the firewall search helps find preexisting items, related work, or internal documents, all of which allow employees to leverage the technology to their advantage and avoid duplicating work.

People expect to find things, and fast—human nature craves simplicity and accuracy.

Definition

Let's look at the definition of search:

To make a thorough examination of, or look over carefully in order to find something.

To make a careful examination or investigation of, to probe. Or to conduct a thorough investigation, seek.

Source: American Heritage Dictionary of the English Language, Fourth Edition (or Google "define:search")

As the definition points out, searching is the action of seeking something, yet the most important part of searching for something is the ability to find it. I've said it several times to multiple search engineers: instead of "search engines," we should call them "find engines," but I have received no traction with this idea.

Semantics aside, this book will focus on Enterprise Search, and specifically with Solr. We define Enterprise Search as **the practice of generating content and making it searchable to a defined audience out of multiple enterprise-type data sources, like a database or a CMS.**

As an example, if you use SharePoint in your organization, the search input found at the top right is classed as an enterprise search solution. Anything that attempts to take a large tangled mass of many different sources of internal corporate data, and allows that data to be indexed, filtered, and organized with a goal to finding inner information easier, is classed as and applicable to be an enterprise based search solution.

Why Solr?

Apache Solr is open-source, it has a fast and sophisticated text search, it's highly extensible, highly scalable, and can work with dynamic content. It has great query speed when properly scaled, and there are many more reasons. Solr also has a very active development community made of individuals and companies who contribute with new features and bug fixes on a regular basis.

On an historic note, search never used to be for the faint of heart. Some of the older solutions were very, very complex and would easily cost many tens of thousands of dollars; a fully commercially supported solution might even cost millions of dollars. Then Solr changed the name of the game in a very big way, and now it's here to stay.

Search engines are a totally different animal. You will either fall in love with what you can do with a search engine, or you might end up absolutely hating them if you try to tackle them head-on without the proper resources. With Solr, you're in luck: this is a proper resource for a small budget with an army of helpers to help you get started smoothly and efficiently.

Solr's History and Famous Sites

Solar (with an A) was developed as an in-house platform by CNET Networks (starting in 2004, by Yonik Seeley) to add search to the company website. In 2006, CNET Networks decided to openly publish the code by donating it to the Apache Foundation under the Lucene top-level project, and it became Solr. In case you are wondering, Solr is not an acronym.

Now, Apache Solr powers some of the biggest enterprise search sites and institutions like the White House, AOL, AT&T Interactive, Yellow Pages, Instagram, Usados.cr, eHarmony, Sears, Netflix, Zappos, Disney, NASA, and many more.

Chapter 2 Architecture of an Enterprise Search Application

Where and How

From an architectural point of view, there are two different areas that need to be discussed. The first one is **where** the search engine fits within your solution, the second one is the **how to** of Solr's architecture.

Placing the Search Engine

Let's take a look at the following figure, something I like to call the search application 10,000-foot view.

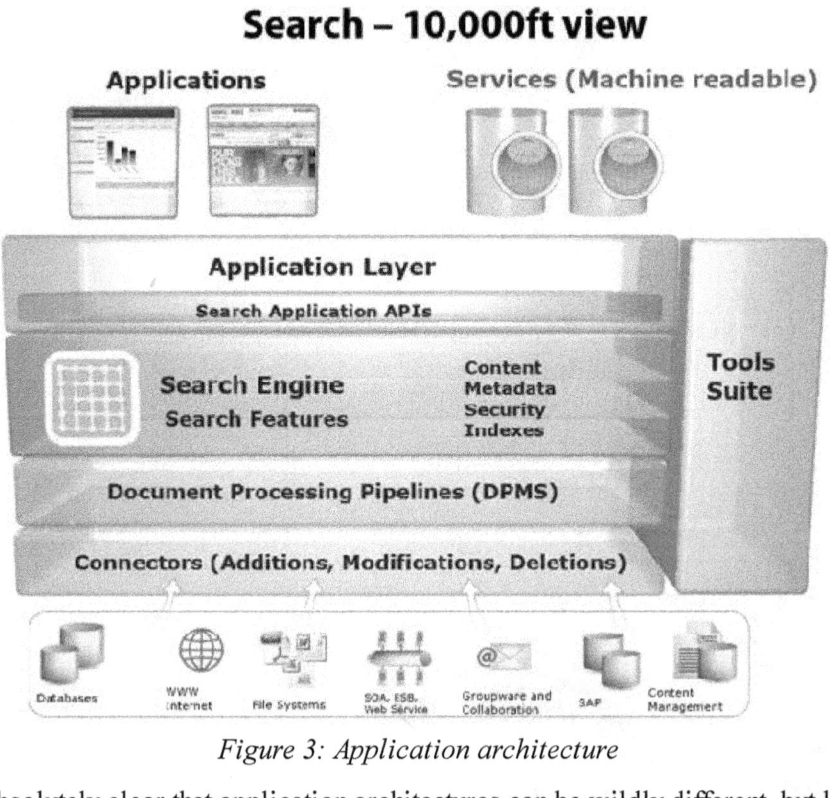

Figure 3: Application architecture

It is absolutely clear that application architectures can be wildly different, but let's make a few assumptions here and generalize to some degree on some of the most general use cases, starting from the top of the diagram.

We can assume that our application will have a UI, which can be built in ASP.NET Web Forms, MVC, AngularJS, PHP, or many other UI frameworks. Our application also has an API that might be used for other applications to connect to, such as an iOS or Android mobile application.

Eventually we get to the application, which may be your key source of income, and you are very proud of it. If you're like I was before I discovered Solr, you probably have something really nice, but that has technical elements that just do not feel right. You may even have provided a not-so-nice user experience that frustrated a few—or even a few thousand—users.

This is where search comes in. You connect to the search engine via the search API. Solr provides an innovative RESTful interface for your needs, or you can choose a client like SolrNet or SolrJ. This all means that your application can run a query or two, refine and provide the user with **Indexes** to the exact resulting **Content**, and through the use of **MetaData** retrieve the required results with the appropriate levels of **Security**.

Let's go to the bottom of the diagram for a moment to understand the multiple data sources that can provide data to your search engine. Most applications get their data from a database, like SQL Server or MySQL. However, in many cases they could also be getting it from a NoSQL database, content source, other applications like a Content Management System, or the file system.

There are multiple ways to retrieve the data that we will be adding to the search engines. One of them is what's called a connector, which retrieves data from the store and provides it to a document-processing pipeline.

The document-processing pipeline, also known as DPMS, takes the content from a data source, performs any necessary transformations, and prepares to feed the data to the search engine.

Inside the Search Engine

Solr is hosted in an application container, which can be either Jetty or Tomcat. For those of you with little to no experience with Jetty or Tomcat, they are web servers just like Internet Information Services (IIS) or nginx.

For development purposes, Solr comes with Jetty out of the box in an extremely easy-to-use, one-line startup command. However, if you wanted to host within Tomcat, you need Solr.war. For those of you that don't know Java, .war stands for Web Application aRchive.

Let's now take a look at the architecture, starting from the bottom.

SOLR Architecture Overview

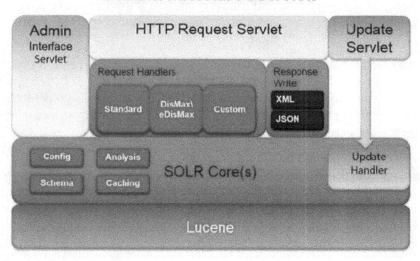

Figure 4: Solr architecture

The first and most important point is that Lucene, a free, open-source information retrieval software library, is the actual search engine that powers Solr. This is such an important point; Solr has actually been made part of the much larger Apache Lucene project.

It really caught my attention when I first discovered Solr within Lucene, so much so that I simply had to investigate it further, and I'm very glad I chose to do so. Lucene is written in Java, was originally created in 1999 by Doug Cutting, and has since been ported to multiple other languages. Solr, however, continues to use the Java version.

There are many other projects that extend and build on Lucene's capabilities. One of these is ElasticSearch, which even makes for a good Solr contender (though arguments are accepted).

On top of Lucene, we have the Solr core, which is running an instance of a Lucene index and logs along with all the Solr configuration files. Queries are formatted and expanded in the way in which Lucene is expecting them, meaning you do not need to do this manually (which can be tedious and complex). These queries are configured and managed (along with how to expand them, and configure the schema details) in the files *schema.xml* and *solrconfig.xml*. In simpler deployments, you can often get away with modifying only these two files. What follows is the very short explanation of the purpose of each one:

- Schema.xml contains all of the details about which fields your documents can contain and how those fields should be accessed with when adding documents to the index or querying those fields.

- Solrconfig.xml is the file that contains most of the parameters for configuring Solr itself.

If you look within Solr Core(s) in the Solr Architecture diagram in Figure 4, you can see where analysis and caching reside. Analysis is in charge of processing fields during either query or indexing time. Caching allows performance improvement.

Initially Solr only supported a single core, but more recent versions can support multiple cores, each one of which will have all the components shown in orange on the architecture diagram. Solr also uses the word "collection" very often; in Solr-speak, a collection is a single index that can be distributed among multiple servers. When you download and start Solr, it comes with a sample index called collection1, which you can also call a core.

To be very clear, let's define some common Solr nomenclature:

- Core: A physical search index.
- Collection: A logical search index that can be made up of multiple cores.

Things get a bit more complex when you introduce SolrCloud Replication and start talking about Shards, Leaders, Replicas, Nodes, Clusters, and ZooKeeper; these, however, are advanced concepts that would belong in a second book about the subject.

Request handlers are responsible for defining the logic executed for any request received by Solr. This includes queries and index updates.

Once a query is received, it is processed by the query parser. There are many parsers available, such as the Standard query parser, DisMax, and eDisMax, which are the most commonly used. You can, however, create your own custom parser if you wish.

In Solr 1.3 and earlier, creating a custom parser was the only way forward. Since version 1.3, DisMax became the default query parser while still maintaining the ability to customize things when needed.

Response writers are in charge of preparing the data in multiple formats to be sent back to the client, for example, in JSON or XML-based data.

The HTTP request servlet is where you connect to Solr, and the update servlet is used to modify your data via the update handler.

 Note: If the term "servlet" is a strange one, don't worry. Think of a servlet as an endpoint on a web server. Servlets are specific to the Java world, and are similar to controllers in other web technologies.

Eventually we reach the admin interface servlet, which provides Solr's default administration UI, something you'll come to rely on once you have deployed your search engine.

We could easily keep peeling away layer after layer and getting into more and more complex and advanced functionality. However, that's not the purpose of this book, so we'll keep the details at a reasonably simple level.

Chapter 3 Solr Configuration

Getting Solr

The first step to get a working installation of Solr is to actually download it, which you can do here. You can also find it by typing "download Solr" into your favorite web search engine.

Figure 5: Solr homepage

Click **Download** so that you are redirected to the appropriate mirror site for downloading Solr's latest version. In this case, since I'm running Windows, I will be downloading the zip file, **solr-4.10.2.zip**. Source code is also available for download in **solr-4.10.2-src.tgz**, and if you need an older version of Apache Solr, you can go to the Apache archives.

The file may take some time to download due to its 150-MB size. While you wait, now is a good time to start checking your prerequisites, mainly Java. In older versions you could run on Java 1.6, but with Solr 4.8 and above, you need Java 7 (hopefully update 55 or later, as there are known bugs in previous versions). At the time of writing of this book, 4.10.2 is Solr's latest version.

To confirm you have the correct Java installed, open the Windows command line, which can be done via the Windows key + **R**, or typing cmd in the Start menu or Run screen. Now, within the command line, please type java -version. The response will tell you which version of Java you are running. A 'java' is not recognized as an internal or external command response means Java is not properly installed. Please go back to Java's installation instructions, making sure the environment variable PATH correctly points to the Java directory. A correct installation will show the following:

```
Microsoft Windows [Version 6.1.7601]
Copyright (c) 2009 Microsoft Corporation.  All rights reserved.

C:\Users\xavier>java -version
java version "1.7.0_67"
Java(TM) SE Runtime Environment (build 1.7.0_67-b01)
Java HotSpot(TM) 64-Bit Server VM (build 24.65-b04, mixed mode)
```

Figure 6: Output that should be seen from running "java -version"

I have Java 1.6 update 67, which means I am good to go.

Once your download is complete, extract all contents into a folder called *c:\solr-succinctly* in the root of your hard drive.

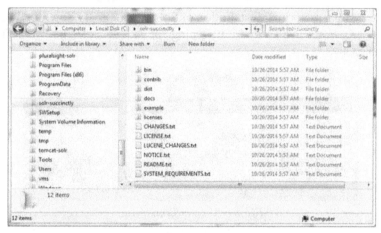

Figure 7: Solr unzipped

In the **solr-succinctly** directory, you will find several folders and files. First, there are a few text files, which include changes, license, notice, readme, and system requirements.

In the **example** folder, you will find a fully self-contained Solr installation. It comes complete with a sample configuration, documents to index, and a web application server called Jetty for running Solr directly out of the box. Remember, if you are a .NET developer, Jetty will be the equivalent of IIS.

The Jetty application web server provided with this distribution is meant for development purposes. However, there are full distributions of the same software available for production use when you reach that point.

In the **dist** folder, you should find a file named **Solr.war**; this is the main Solr application that you deploy to your application server in order to run Apache Solr. This folder also contains many useful JAR files. To clarify, a JAR (Java Archive) is a package file format typically used to aggregate many Java class files and associated metadata and resources (such as text, images, etc.) into one file to distribute application software or libraries on the Java platform.

In the **contrib** folder, you should find Solr's contribution modules. As with many open source projects, what you'll find in here are extensions to Solr. The runnable Java files for each of these contrib modules are actually in the **dist** folder.

In the **docs** folder, you'll find HTML files and assets that will increase your understanding of Solr. You'll find a good, quick tutorial, and of course, Solr's core API documentation.

I've seen a few people copy only the **example** folder to get Solr started, especially during local deployments for development. It works, but will present you with a number of problems, as there are dependencies that you'll almost definitely need to make things run correctly. It's always best to copy the entire contents of the downloaded zip file. Paths are relative, however, meaning you can easily rename **example** to something more meaningful without causing any significant issues.

For my purposes throughout this book, I'll rename my cloned folder **succinctly**.

Starting Solr

Now that we have Solr, let's fire it up and get the party started!

At this point you might be expecting a **solrinstaller.exe**. This is not how it works. It is a bit different, although not complicated at all.

We're now ready to run the Solr development environment using the included application web server Jetty. A word of advice: Jetty is included with Solr, but it is not the only option. I also use Tomcat for production purposes, and there are other alternatives. The bundled-in Jetty just makes it a lot simpler to get started quickly.

I am using Windows right now, but the process is very similar in other operating systems.

The steps are extremely simple:

1. Open the command line, which can be done by typing cmd in the Windows Run dialog. The Run dialog can be displayed with the Windows key + R.
2. Change the folder to the one you created previously, where you extracted Solr. Then, go into the **succinctly** folder, which you recently cloned from **example**.
3. Now run java -jar start.jar. If all goes as expected, the console will start loading. Initialization steps will be displayed in the command line; please expect a large of amount of text to be shown. This is normal.

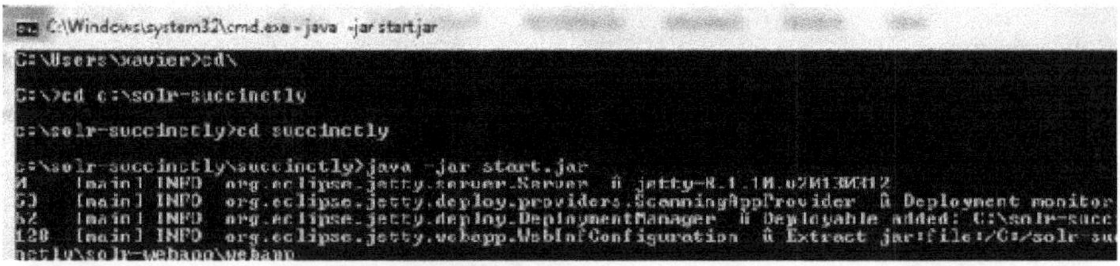

Figure 8: Starting Solr

4. And finally, the most important part of the setup: open a browser and navigate to http://localhost:8983/solr. If you see the following, you should be smiling, because you have Apache Solr running:

Figure 9: Solr up and running

If you don't see the screen in Figure 9 in your browser, or if Solr does not load, please review the text output in your console. Exceptions are visible in the messages —though sometimes they are hard to find. The most likely scenario where Solr will not load is if there are errors in the configuration files, most likely due to changes that have been made while experimenting.

Configuring Solr in a Different Port

Now it's time to learn how to make configuration changes to Solr. For our first example, we will perform a very simple change to run it from a different network port. This change is a common scenario, and usually required for things like corporate firewall rules. The following steps will guide you through this process:

1. Navigate to the **etc** folder using Windows Explorer.
2. Open the **jetty.xml** configuration file with your text editor of choice. Notepad++ is a good recommendation.
3. Look for the word *port* and within the node `<New class="org.eclipse.jetty.server.bio.SocketConnector">` you will see a subnode with the default port 8983. Please make sure you are replacing the correct one, which is not commented out.
4. Change it to 8984.
5. Go back to the Admin UI, modify your URL to point to the new port, and refresh.

This webpage is not available

Figure 10: Solr in another port

As you can see, the new port is not yet working as expected. You need to restart Solr. This is **NOT** a hot swap change!

To stop the current Solr instance, you need to change to the window where you started Solr, and then press **Ctrl + C** so the service shuts down. Then restart using the same command as before, `java-jar start.jar`. Solr will start. Now, if you refresh your browser, once again you'll see Apache Solr, easy as that.

Figure 11: Restarting Solr

At this point I will revert back to using 8983, the default port, and restart Solr. These steps apply only when using Jetty as an application web container. If you use Tomcat or another container, you'll need to use different configuration instructions.

Solr's Admin UI

Solr features a web interface that makes it easy for administrators and programmers to view the Solr configuration details, run queries, analyze document fields, and fine-tune a Solr instance, as well as access online documentation and help. As shown in Figure 12, the admin section is made up of the sections Dashboard, Logging, Core Admin, Java Properties, and Thread Dump. There's also core selector (a drop-down list) with multiple different functionalities, and the main working pane to the right of the menu.

Figure 12: Solr menu

If you've already pointed your browser at http://localhost:8983/solr, then you're ready to review each section in turn.

Getting Assistance

Underneath the main work pane, you'll see a small, icon-driven menu.

The main objective of this menu is to give you quick access to the various help and assistance resources available to Solr users. It is made up of the documentation, which is hosted here, and has links pointing to the official issue tracker located on the JIRA network. There's also a link to the Solr IRC channel, the community forum, and the Solr query syntax guide, all of which is going to be very useful.

Figure 13: Solr's working pane menu

Dashboard

The Dashboard is the default section that is loaded when you navigate to the Admin UI. It displays information it collects on your Instance, System, and Java Virtual Machine (JVM). Depending on your configuration, it has been observed that the memory graph may not display information when Windows virtual memory is set to automatic, or when the system is configured not to use Swap memory.

Logging

The Logging section displays messages from Solr's log file. When you start Solr, you only have one core, but if you have multiple cores, then all of the messages will be displayed.

Figure 14: Solr Logging

Underneath the Logging menu item, you see the hierarchy of class maps and class names for your instance. Click the column at the right and select the logging level from All, Trace, Debug, Info, Warn, Error, Fatal, Off, and Unset as shown in Figure 15.

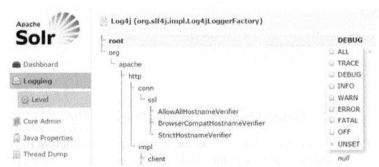

Figure 15: Solr Logging hierarchy

Core Admin

As you might remember from a previous section, we mentioned Lucene cores. A core is a full copy of a Lucene index with its own schema and configuration.

You can manage your cores in the core admin section. The buttons at the top allow you to add a core, unload one of the existing cores, rename a core, swap a core, reload the core with any changes made since the last reload, and optimize a core.

Figure 16: Core admin

💡 *Tip: When you click the Reload button, you have to wait for the button to turn green, or your changes will not take effect. The commands here are the same ones available through the core admin handler, but they are provided in a way that is easy to work with. If there are problems loading the core, you will see the exceptions in the log, or if you started from the console, the commands will also be displayed there. Restarting Solr will also load all cores, including new ones.*

Java Properties

The Java Properties screen allows easy, read-only access to one of the most essential components of a top-performing Solr system. It allows you to see all the properties of the JVM running Solr, including the class paths, file encodings, JVM memory settings, operating system, and more.

Figure 17: Java Properties Thread Dump

The Thread Dump screen lets you inspect the threads currently active in your server. Each thread is listed, and access to the stack traces is available where applicable. There's also an icon that indicates state; for example, a green check mark signifies a runnable state. The available states are new, runnable, locked, waiting, time waiting, and terminated.

Core Selector

The core selector allows you to select or find a specific core. Click **Core Selector**, and a drop-down menu will appear. You can start typing your core's name, which comes in handy when you have many cores, or you can click the name of your desired core. Once you have selected your core, you'll be able to perform core-specific functions. When you click on the core, it will start by displaying the Overview with the statistics for this particular core.

Figure 19: Core drop-down menu

Analysis

The Analysis screen lets you inspect how your data will be handled during either indexing or query time, according to the field, field type, and dynamic role configurations found in the schema.xml. Ideally, you would want content to be handled consistently, and this screen allows you to validate them in the field type or field analysis chains.

This screen is also very useful for development when selecting analyzers for debugging purposes. Analyzers will be mentioned later in this book.

Figure 20: Analysis

DataImport

Some of the most common data sources include XML files and relational databases. Therefore, we need an easy way to import from databases and XML files into Solr.

This is achieved using the DIH or data import handler. It is a contrib that provides a configuration-driven way to import data into Solr in both full builds and incremental delta imports. The DIH within the admin UI shows you the information about the current statuses of the data import handler.

In the current instance, there are no data import handlers configured, and they will not be covered in this book. However, if you want to learn how to configure and use data import handlers, your current Solr download comes with a predefined example that is easy to start and test. Please go to the **example-DIH** folder in **C:\solr-succinctly\example** and open **Readme.txt**. Follow the instructions you find there to get started.

Documents

The Documents screen allows you to execute multiple Solr indexing commands in a variety of formats directly from the browser. It allows you to copy or upload documents, JSON, CSV, and XML and submit them to the index. You can also construct documents by selecting fields and field values. You should always start by defining a request handler to use by typing the name of the handler in the *Request-Handler (qt)* textbox. By default, */update* will be defined.

Figure 21: Request handler

Files

The Files screen is used to browse and view the various configuration files for a specific core (for example, solrconfig.xml and schema.xml). It is read-only, and it is a great way to access your files without having to actually log into the machine.

Figure 22: Files screen

Ping

You can ping a specific core and determine if it is active. It is very simple to use; simply click this option, and it tells you how many milliseconds it took for it to respond.

Plugins and Stats

The Plugins and Stats display shows statistics like the status and performance of the caches, searches, and configuration of handlers for both search as well as request handlers. A snapshot is taken when the page is loaded, and you can either watch changes or refresh the values by clicking on the marked menu items.

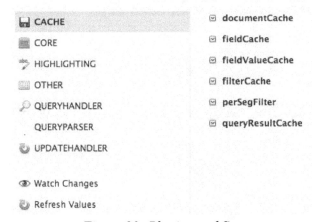

Figure 23: Plugins and Stats

Query

The Query section is probably one of the most important parts of the admin UI. It's where you submit a structured query and analyze the results. The Admin UI includes a set of options for the multiple available parameters to make the user's life simpler, including:

- **request-Handler(qt):** Specifies the request handler to use; it uses the standard if it's not specified.
- **q:** The query, for which results returned will be ranked from more relevant to least relevant.
- **fq:** The filter query, basically used to narrow down result sets. The difference with q is that fq does not affect ranking.
- **sort:** Tells Solr by which field you want sorting to be applied, either ascending or descending.
- **start, rows:** Controls how many results and starting where should be returned.

Used mainly for paging.

- **fl:** Specifies which fields should be returned in the response. If not specified, all are returned. In Solr 4 and above, you can specify functions (a more advanced topic).

- **df:** The default field; it will only take effect if the qf (Query Fields) is not defined.

- **wt:** The response writer, which indicates how to format the response; for example, XML or JSON.

- **indent:** Makes it more readable.

- **debugQuery:** Used to display debug information

- **dismax:** Ticking this checkbox displays the DisMax query parser parameter. DisMax is already the default query parser in newer versions of Solr.

- **edismax:** Displays the Extended Dismax Parameters, which is an extended query parser used to overcome the limitations of DisMax.

- **hl:** Enables highlighting of results.

- **facet:** Displays faceting parameter options.

- **spatial:** Shows options for spatial or geo-spatial search.

- **spellcheck:** Enables spell checking of results.

If an option is not available in the Admin UI, there are always the "Raw Query Parameters," which basically just pass along the specified parameters to Solr verbatim.

The options I just mentioned will be covered more in Chapter 8.

When you execute a query within the Admin UI, the results will load in the right-most panel. This makes it very simple to run queries, review results, tweak, and run queries again.

Depending on your browser and configuration, one tip that I have for you is to open the results within the browser and use XML instead of JSON. I normally use Google Chrome, and the browser presents the XML in such a way so that you can expand and contract each section, making it easy to view all results. Simply click the box with a link above the results that looks like the one shown in Figure 24:

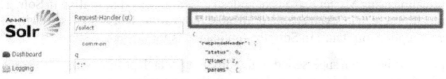

Figure 24: Click to open query

Now let's take a quick look at a response, which is made up of several sections that can include the following:

- **Response header:** Includes the status, the query time, and the parameters.
- **Results:** Includes the documents returned from the search engine that match the query in doc subsections.
- **Facets:** Items or search results grouped into categories that allow users to refine or drill down in specific search results. Each facet also displays number of hits within the search that match each specific category.

I encourage you to play around and experiment with the query section; this is where you learn the most about Solr.

The following figure shows you how a typical response might look:

```
▼<response>
  ▼<lst name="responseHeader">
      <int name="status">0</int>
      <int name="QTime">16</int>
    ▼<lst name="params">
        <str name="indent">true</str>
        <str name="q">*:*</str>
        <str name="qt">usados</str>
        <str name="wt">xml</str>
        <str name="rows">5</str>
      </lst>
    </lst>
  ▼<result name="response" numFound="603" start="0" maxScore="1.0">
    ▶<doc>...</doc>
    ▶<doc>...</doc>
    ▶<doc>...</doc>
    ▶<doc>...</doc>
    ▶<doc>...</doc>
    </result>
  ▼<lst name="facet_counts">
      <lst name="facet_queries"/>
    ▶<lst name="facet_fields">...</lst>
      <lst name="facet_dates"/>
      <lst name="facet_ranges"/>
    </lst>
  </response>
```

Figure 25: Example of a Solr response

Replication

Replication using Master and Slave nodes is the old method of scaling in Solr. The replication screen lets you enable or disable replication. It also shows you the current replication status; in Solr, the replication is for the index only.

Replication has been superseded with SolrCloud, which provides the functionality required to scale a Solr solution. However, if you're still using index replication, you can use this screen to see the replication state.

Schema Browser

The Schema browser displays schema data. It loads a specific field when opened from the analysis window, or, if you open it directly, you can select a field or field type. If you click on the load term info, it will show you the top end terms that are in the index for that field. And if you click on a term, you will be taken to the query screen to see the results of a query of that term in that field.

You can load the term information for a field if there are terms for that specific field. A histogram will show the number of terms with a given frequency in that field. This may be a bit confusing in the beginning, but later on it will be pretty useful.

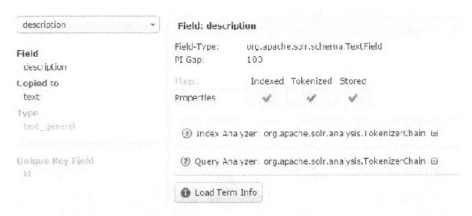

Figure 26: Schema browser

Summary

We have concluded the quick tour of the Admin UI. The objective was to provide you with an overview of the many different components of the Admin UI, and explain what are they used for.

The next step in this journey is to move on to understanding how we model our data according to Solr's needs, and for this purpose, we will use the sample data provided.

Chapter 4 Your First Index

Solr's Sample Data

At this point, you should have a running Solr instance and a good understanding of the tooling available to you in the Admin UI. Now, it's time to start making Solr work for us.

Start by opening a command prompt and navigating to the `exampledocs` folder located within **C:\solr-succinctly\succinctly**. If you shut down your Solr, start it again with `java -jar start.jar`. Make sure you do this in a different command prompt, however, as you'll need to type in the first one while Solr is running.

Within `exampledocs`, there are several CSV and XML files with sample data ready to be indexed and the distribution includes a simple command line tool for POSTing data to Solr, called *post.jar*. For instructions and examples on usage, use the following command:

```
Java -jar post.jar -help
```

```
Examples:
    java -jar post.jar *.xml
    java -Ddata=args  -jar post.jar '<delete><id>42</id></delete>'
    java -Ddata=stdin -jar post.jar < hd.xml
    java -Ddata=web -jar post.jar http://example.com/
    java -Dtype=text/csv -jar post.jar *.csv
    java -Dtype=application/json -jar post.jar *.json
    java -Durl=http://localhost:8983/solr/update/extract -Dparams=lit
    java -Dauto -jar post.jar *
    java -Dauto -Drecursive -jar post.jar afolder
    java -Dauto -Dfiletypes=ppt,html -jar post.jar afolder
```

Figure 27: Help for post.jar

Before we start indexing any documents, let's first confirm that we don't have any documents in the index. One way to do so is to navigate to the Admin UI, chose `collection1` from the Core Selector, and click on **Query**. Then, at the bottom of the section, click **Execute Query** or click on any of the non-multiline text boxes, and push Enter.

All-in-all this constitutes quite a few steps—there is, however, a quicker way. Navigate directly to Solr via its RESTful interface, querying for all documents. This will not use the Admin UI; it will just run the query. The URL looks like this:

http://localhost:8983/solr/collection1/select?q=*%3A*&wt=json&indent=true

As you can see in the results, we have zero documents in our index.

```
"response": {
    "numFound": 0,
    "start": 0,
    "docs": []
}
```

Figure 28: No documents in the index

Time to upload the sample data. From `exampledocs` in your command prompt, type:

```
Java -jar post.jar *.xml
```

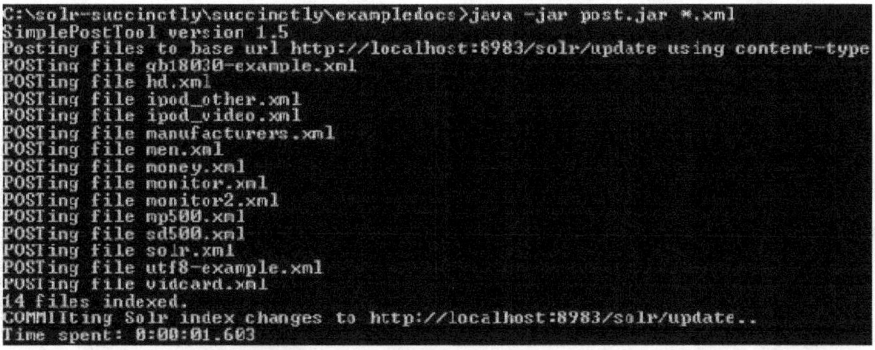

Figure 29: POST example files

All the XML files supplied have been posted directly into my index and have been committed; this has all been done automatically by the POST tool. It's also worth noting that a simple mistake that many people make is they post data to the index, but forget to commit. Data is only ever available for searching if you remember to execute the commit; however, since the post tool does this for you automatically, it's a mistake you often won't make.

Post.jar is only one way of indexing documents. Another mechanism is the data import handler, which allows connections to databases and imports data in either full or incremental crawls. You can also add XML, JSON, CSV, or other types of files via the Documents section in the Admin UI. Additionally, you can use a client library, like SolrNet or SolrJ, and there are multiple content-processing tools that post documents to the Solr index. One that I see being used all the time is Search Technology's ASPIRE, which has a PostToSolr functionality.

Switch back to your browser and run the default query again. You should now see 32 documents in your index. The following figure shows the output you should now get, allowing you to become familiar with Solr responses.

```
▼<response>
  ▼<lst name="responseHeader">
     <int name="status">0</int>
     <int name="QTime">1</int>
   ▼<lst name="params">
      <str name="indent">true</str>
      <str name="q">*:*</str>
      <str name="wt">xml</str>
     </lst>
  </lst>
  ▼<result name="response" numFound="32" start="0">
    ▼<doc>
       <str name="id">GB18030TEST</str>
       <str name="name">Test with some GB18030 encoded characters</str>
     ▼<arr name="features">
         <str>No accents here</str>
         <str>这是一个功能</str>
         <str>This is a feature (translated)</str>
         <str>这份文件是很有光泽</str>
         <str>This document is very shiny (translated)</str>
       </arr>
       <float name="price">0.0</float>
       <str name="price_c">0,USD</str>
       <bool name="inStock">true</bool>
       <long name="_version_">1487804614883409920</long>
     </doc>
```

Figure 30: Example documents indexed

At this point, you've run a couple of queries, which amounts to asking your search engine to perform a basic query. You did this in two ways: first by using the Query section in the Admin UI, and second by using Solr's RESTful interface.

http://localhost:8983/solr/collection1/select?q=*%3A*&wt=json&indent=true

Figure 31: Solr query

Simple Anatomy of a Query and a Response

Query

If you select a core, click **Query**, and press **Enter**, you will be able to see a query and a response. In this section, we'll start to really understand what is actually happening by using the sample data we just uploaded into collection1.

> *Tip: If your browser supports XML formatting (like Google Chrome does), you can make a quick change for easier readability. Please open the response in your browser, look for the wt=json parameter in the URL, and change to wt=xml. The wt is the response writer, which tells Solr how to format the response. Try it.*

As we've seen so far, Solr uses a fairly standard RESTful interface, which allows you to easily see the URL used to make a query; like any standard URL, it's made up of the host name, the port number, and the application name.

The request handler for queries (in this case we're using select) is the default request handler, and is the Solr equivalent of "Hello World." The default query of exampledocs is made up of the following URL parameters:

URL	Description
http://localhost:8983/solr	This is the URL where Solr is hosted.
/collection1	The second part of the URL indicates the collection that you are currently working on. Given that you can have multiple collections within a server, you need to specify which one you want to use. Believe it or not, at some point Solr could host only one collection.
/select?	The next URL part indicates which request handler you are using. Select is the default handler used for searching. You can also use /update when you want to modify data instead of querying. It is possible to create your own according to your needs.

q=*%3A*&wt=json&indent=true	Everything after the ? are the query parameters. Like any URL text, it needs to be properly escaped, using correct URL encoding rules.

Like with any technology, the best way to learn and understand is to play with it; imagine Solr's default install as your big data and enterprise search training wheels. Open the Admin UI, change the parameters, and see how your results are modified and what differences your changes make to the search. Once you've tried a few queries and gotten a feel for how they work, you're ready to move on.

Response

When you run a query, the response you get will contain two full sections:

- ResponseHeader
- Response

You can see an example in the following figure:

```
▼<response>
  ►<lst name="responseHeader">...</lst>
  ►<result name="response" numFound="32" start="0">...</result>
</response>
```

Figure 32: Solr response

The ResponseHeader contains information about the response itself. The status tells you the outcome; o stands for *OK*. If you query for a nonexistent request handler, you would get a 404 response code as the HTTP response.

The ResponseHeader also includes QTime, which is the query execution time and echoing of the parameters.

```
▼<lst name="responseHeader">
   <int name="status">0</int>
   <int name="QTime">2</int>
   ▼<lst name="params">
     <str name="q">*:*</str>
     <str name="indent">true</str>
     <str name="wt">xml</str>
   </lst>
 </lst>
```

Figure 33: Response header

The response section includes the results of those documents that matched your query in *doc* subsections or nodes. It includes a numFound that indicates how many documents matched your query, and *start,* which is used for paging.

Other Response Sections

- **highlighting:** Allows fragments of documents that match the user's query to be displayed in the response.

- **facet_counts:** Shows the facets that have been constructed for the result list, including the facet fields and facet values (with counts) to populate each field.

- **spellcheck:** Will include suggestions for possible misspellings in the user's query.

- **debug:** Intended for development and debugging. Only included if specified as part of the query. Among its subsections, it includes `explain` to understand how each document scored according to the in-relevancy ranking algorithm, and `timing` to understand how long each component took for processing. In `parsedquery`, it displays how the query string is submitted to the query parser.

```
▼<result name="response" numFound="32" start="0">
  ▼<doc>
      <str name="id">GB18030TEST</str>
      <str name="name">Test with some GB18030 encoded characters</str>
    ▼<arr name="features">
        <str>No accents here</str>
        <str>这是一个功能</str>
        <str>This is a feature (translated)</str>
        <str>这份文件是很有光泽</str>
        <str>This document is very shiny (translated)</str>
      </arr>
      <float name="price">0.0</float>
      <str name="price_c">0,USD</str>
      <bool name="inStock">true</bool>
      <long name="_version_">1488235981567950848</long>
  </doc>
  ▶<doc>...</doc>
```

Figure 34: A Solr document

Docs and Modeling Your Data

You are probably wondering at this point how we model our data within Solr. That's where one of the main configuration files comes into play—you model your data and specify to Solr how to handle it in the Schema.xml file. The following figure shows an example.

```
<field name="id" type="string" indexed="true" stored="true" required="true" multiValued="false" />

<field name="sku" type="text_en_splitting_tight" indexed="true" stored="true" omitNorms="true"/>
<field name="name" type="text_general" indexed="true" stored="true"/>
<field name="manu" type="text_general" indexed="true" stored="true" omitNorms="true"/>
<field name="cat" type="string" indexed="true" stored="true" multiValued="true"/>
<field name="features" type="text_general" indexed="true" stored="true" multiValued="true"/>
<field name="includes" type="text_general" indexed="true" stored="true" termVectors="true"
       termPositions="true" termOffsets="true" />

<field name="weight" type="float" indexed="true" stored="true"/>
<field name="price" type="float" indexed="true" stored="true"/>
<field name="popularity" type="int" indexed="true" stored="true" />
<field name="inStock" type="boolean" indexed="true" stored="true" />

<field name="store" type="location" indexed="true" stored="true"/>
```

Figure 35: Example docs schema

Each document has a set of fields, and each field can be of a different type. In this specific sample case for the documents we just uploaded, we can see that we have `id`, `sku`, `name`, `manu`, `cat`, `features`, `includes`, `weight`, `price`, `popularity`, `inStock`, and `store`.

The schema also includes a series of common metadata fields, named specifically to match up with Solr Cell metadata.

 Note: Solr Cell is a functionality that allows sending rich documents such as Word or PDF documents directly to Solr for parsing, extraction, and indexing for search. We will not be covering SolrCell in this book.

To use an analogy: if you are familiar with databases, then a doc would correspond to a row. The name would be the column name, and type is exactly the same thing—it indicates what type of information will be stored in this specific field. Required indicates if it is mandatory, just like specifying *NOT NULL* in the structured query language.

The ID in this specific case is just like the primary key, the unique id for the document. It is not absolutely required, but highly recommended. You specify which field you want to be the primary key in the schema in `<uniquekey>`.

```
<uniqueKey>id</uniqueKey>
```

Figure 36: Unique key ID

And now let's get to some specifics:

- Indexed="true|false" is used to specify that this specific field is searchable. It has to be added to the index to be searchable.
- Stored="true|false" can be hard to swallow at first. If you specify that a field is not stored, then whenever you run a query, the original value of that field is not returned. There is, however, one point that is very important. You can set a field to stored="false" and indexed="true", meaning that you index the data, but the data itself for that field is not saved in Solr, so you can't extract it as part of the results.

 Note: While this might seem counter-intuitive, there's actually a pretty simple reason for it. Let's imagine you have some very large fields and you don't care about retrieving the full text; e.g. finding which documents contain the specific terms searched. This gives you a very fast search solution with a very low memory footprint, allowing the client to retrieve the larger amount of data at his own discretion.

- Multivalued="true|false" indicates whether you want to hold multiple fields within the same field. For example, if a book has multiple authors, all of them would be stored in one field.

Solr supports many different data types, which are included in the Solr runtime

packages. If you want to get very technical, they are located in the
org.apache.solr.schema package.

Here is the list according to Solr's wiki:

- BCDIntField
- BCDLongField
- BCDStrField
- BinaryField
- BoolField
- ByteField
- CollationField
- CurrencyField
- DateField
- DoubleField
- EnumField
- ExternalFileField

- FloatField
- ICUCollationField
- IntField
- LatLonType
- LongField
- PointType
- PreAnalyzedField
- RandomSortField
- ShortField
- SortableDoubleField
- SortableFloatField
- SortableIntField

- SortableLongField
- SpatialRecursivePrefixTreeFie
- StrField
- TextField
- TrieDateField
- TrieDoubleField
- TrieField
- TrieFloatField
- TrieIntField
- TrieLongField
- UUIDField

It is worth mentioning that there is something called Schemaless mode, which pretty
much allows for you to add data without the need to model it, as well as dynamic
fields. We will not be covering them in this book.

Playing Around with Solr

With our first Solr "Hello World" query, we simply looked for *:*, meaning all
values for all fields, which returned all 32 documents. Let's raise the stakes a notch
and play around with a few queries, changing different parameters as we go. We
won't get too complicated; we'll just show a few examples to help you understand
some of the basic functionalities of Solr.

A "Real" Query with Facets

In this example, we will run a specific query of *:* and ask for facets to be included.

Using the cores dropdown menu in the Admin UI, select the **collection1** core, type in
video in the **q** field, check **facet**, and select **xml** as the response writer (**wt**). Type in
manu as the facet field and execute the query using the **Execute Query** button.

It should look like this:

Figure 37: Running a query

Two things should definitively stand out from the response. First, you will see only relevant results; in this case, three documents matched instead of 32.

```
<result name="response" numFound="3" start="0">
```

Figure 38: Three documents found

More importantly, you can now see facets for `manu`. We will get into more details later about facets, but for now please take a look at the list within `facet_fields` called `manu`, which holds the list of all manufacturers, sorted from highest occurrence to lowest. It includes the names and a count. Facets are also called navigators, and they allow drill down on specific result sets. In this example, given that the list is very long, I have included an ellipsis (…) to indicate that there are many more results, mainly with 0 values; you can see this reflected in the figure below.

```
<lst name="facet_counts">
  <lst name="facet_queries"/>
  <lst name="facet_fields">
    <lst name="manu">
      <int name="computer">2</int>
      <int name="inc">2</int>
      <int name="apple">1</int>
      <int name="asus">1</int>
      <int name="ati">1</int>
      <int name="technologies">1</int>
      <int name="a">0</int>
      <int name="america">0</int>
        ...
      <int name="viewsonic">0</int>
    </lst>
  </lst>
  <lst name="facet_dates"/>
  <lst name="facet_ranges"/>
  <lst name="facet_intervals"/>
</lst>
```

Figure 39: Facets

Fields

At the present moment we are returning all fields, which may or may not make sense, depending on your specific needs. If you need to provide all fields back to the application, then there is no need to use fl (fields) input. If you want smaller responses to help with performance, especially when using large documents, just include the list of fields that you want returned in fl. Simply type them in separated by a blank space or comma. This also helps with readability while querying for testing.

Figure 40: Returning specific fields

A very neat and useful trick is to include *score* as a field, which will tell you the score (or how relevant a document is) from the result set. Try adding a query to the previous search; I will add q=drive, include the score field, and execute and analyze the results, as you can see in the fl field in the following figure.

Figure 41: Include Score as a Field

Results are ranked from highest to lowest score, or most relevant to least relevant. That is, of course, if no other sorting is applied.

Sorting

To take advantage of the ability to select which fields to display, let's try sort. Sorting to a query is a very simple process—simply type in the field you want to sort on, and then either asc (ascending) or desc (descending), as the next figures demonstrate.

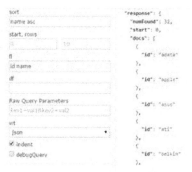

Figure 42: Sorting ascending

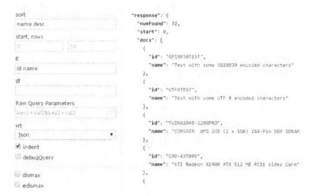

Figure 43: Sorting descending

You can also sort on more than one field at a time. To do this, simply specify the field name, the sort direction, and then separate the groups with a comma. For example: `name desc, id asc.`

Paging: Start and Rows

You can add paging to your applications using Start and Rows. Start is the offset of the first record that you are returning. For example, if you run a query, 10 results are returned by default. You know that you want the second page, so you run the same query, but with start=11 and rows=10, thus producing the second page also containing 10 results.[1]

Learning the Difference between Queries (q) and Filter Queries (fq)

I have already mentioned how q calculates results based on relevancy, and fq is only used to drill down. I also mentioned that fq is very efficient in terms of performance; the reason for this is that filter queries cache results and only stores ids, making access very fast. Now that we've learned how to get a score for our results, we can prove that this is indeed the case.

The steps to do this are very simple:

1. Open two windows, and in each one, navigate in the Admin UI to the query section of collection1. You will be running in both windows. Write down drive and include the following four fields in the `fl` section: id name cat score. For readability, if your browser supports nice XML formatting, please change `wt` to `xml`.

```
<result name="response" numFound="3" start="0" maxScore="0.81656027">
  <doc>
    <str name="id">6H500F0</str>
    <str name="name">Maxtor DiamondMax 11 - hard drive - 500 GB - SATA-300</str>
    <arr name="cat">
      <str>electronics</str>
      <str>hard drive</str>
    </arr>
    <float name="score">0.81656027</float></doc>
  <doc>
    <str name="id">SP2514N</str>
    <str name="name">Samsung SpinPoint P120 SP2514N - hard drive - 250 GB - ATA-133</str>
    <arr name="cat">
      <str>electronics</str>
      <str>hard drive</str>
    </arr>
    <float name="score">0.6804669</float></doc>
  <doc>
    <str name="id">0579B002</str>
    <str name="name">Canon PIXMA MP500 All-In-One Photo Printer</str>
    <arr name="cat">
      <str>electronics</str>
      <str>multifunction printer</str>
      <str>printer</str>
      <str>scanner</str>
      <str>copier</str>
    </arr>
    <float name="score">0.33681393</float></doc>
</result>
```

Figure 44: Query for drive

2. When you execute the query you will get three results, two of which have a category of "hard drive."

We just ran a query using the q field. Let's now run a new query using fq instead. The intention is to prove how q and fq affect queries in a different way. The bottom line is that q affects ranking, while fq does not. It is extremely important to understand this difference, as using them incorrectly will bring results that are not as relevant as they should be.

Query

Please reload the Admin UI in both windows so that we can start from clean query pages.

In one of the windows, add in the q input box the following query: drive AND cat:"hard drive". Be careful with capitalization, and remember to include the following four fields in the fl section: id name cat score. Your query should look like the following.

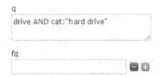

Figure 45: No filter query

Your result should look like this:

```
<result name="response" numFound="2" start="0" maxScore="3.035773">
  <doc>
    <str name="id">6H500F0</str>
    <str name="name">Maxtor DiamondMax 11 - hard drive - 500 GB - SATA-300</str>
    <arr name="cat">
      <str>electronics</str>
      <str>hard drive</str>
    </arr>
    <float name="score">3.035773</float></doc>
  <doc>
    <str name="id">SP2514N</str>
    <str name="name">Samsung SpinPoint P120 SP2514N - hard drive - 250 GB - ATA-133</str>
    <arr name="cat">
      <str>electronics</str>
      <str>hard drive</str>
    </arr>
    <float name="score">2.9439263</float></doc>
</result>
</response>
```

Figure 46: No filter query response

Filter Query

In the other window, set q=drive and add cat:"hard drive" within fq. As before, include the four fields in the fl section: id name cat score. Your query should match the following:

Figure 47: Query and filter query

You will get the following result:

```
<result name="response" numFound="2" start="0" maxScore="0.81656027">
  <doc>
    <str name="id">6H500F0</str>
    <str name="name">Maxtor DiamondMax 11 - hard drive - 500 GB - SATA-300</str>
    <arr name="cat">
      <str>electronics</str>
      <str>hard drive</str>
    </arr>
    <float name="score">0.81656027</float></doc>
  <doc>
    <str name="id">SP2514N</str>
    <str name="name">Samsung SpinPoint P120 SP2514N - hard drive - 250 GB - ATA-133</str>
    <arr name="cat">
      <str>electronics</str>
      <str>hard drive</str>
    </arr>
    <float name="score">0.6804669</float></doc>
</result>
</response>
```

Figure 48: Query and filter query response

When you look at the response results, using '`fq`' doesn't affect the score. The first run took the longest, and the second was quicker. The third run using '`fq`' has not changed at all, showing that Solr has just returned the results already cached from the previous queries.

Element/Score	q=drive	q=drive& fq=cat="hard drive"	q=drive AND cat="hard drive"
6H500F0	0.81656027	0.81656027	3.035773
SP2514N	0.6804669	0.6804669	2.9439263
0579B002	0.33681393	--	--

Summary

In this chapter, you've learned how to load Solr's sample documents and how to run a few simple queries. We've discussed the anatomy of a simple query and response, and finally, proved the difference between q and fq in terms of ranking. In the next chapter, we'll continue by learning how to create a schema for our own documents.

Chapter 5 Schema.xml: The Content

Have you ever heard of the learning triangle? It basically states that the level of mastery on any specific topic increases as you go through the following process: reading, seeing, hearing, watching, doing, and teaching. You are reading this right now, but to maximize the learning process, I encourage you to follow along in your own Solr installation.

In this chapter, we will create our own example using real-life data: a list of books in the Syncfusion *Succinctly* Series. It's not a large set of data, but it'll do just fine for me to demonstrate the steps required to index your own content.

Our Own Example

I chose the *Succinctly* series because it is something that I identify with, and it is easy to understand. We will take the library and create an application to index the books, and allow people to browse them via tags or by text searching. Let's get this party started!

Figure 49: Syncfusion Succinctly Series

We will start by indexing data for only three fields, and then over the course of the chapter, incrementally add a few more so we can perform queries with faceting, dates, multi-values, and other features that you would most likely need in your application. Let's take a quick look at our sample data to see what it contains. As you can see, we have things like book title, description, and author. We will be using a CSV file; however, for display, I am currently showing you the data using Excel.

bookid	title	description	author	tags
1	jQuery Succinctly	jQuery Succinctly was written to express, in short order, the concepts	Cody Lindley	jquery
2	Git Succinctly	Get up and running with one of the fastest-spreading revision control	Ryan Hodson	git|source-control
3	PDF Succinctly	A primer for understanding the components of PDFs, how text and	Ryan Hodson	pdf
4	HTTP Succinctly	Learn to write better web apps and services, and debug them when	Scott Allen	http|web-apps|services
5	JavaScript Succinctly	If you're an intermediate JavaScript developer, JavaScript Succinctly is the book for you.	Cody Lindley	javascript

Figure 50: Sample data

Whenever you want to add fields to your index, you need to tell Solr the name, type, and a couple of other attributes so that it knows what to do with them. In layman's terms, you define the structure of the data of the index.

You do this by using the Schema.xml file. This file is usually the first one you configure when setting up a new installation. In it you declare your fields, field types, and attributes. You specify how to treat each field when documents are added to or queried from the index, if they are required or multi-valued, and whether they need to be stored or used for searching. Even though it is not required, you can also declare which one is your primary key for each document (which needs to be unique). One very important thing to remember is that it's not advisable to change the schema after documents have been added to the index, so try to make sure you have everything you need before adding it.

If you look at the schema.xml provided in your download, you'll see it includes the following sections:

Version

The version number tells Solr how to treat some of the attributes in the schema. The current version is 1.5 as of Solr 4.10, and you should not change this version in your application.

```
<schema name="example" version="1.5">
```

Figure 51: Version number

Type Definitions

Logically there are two types: simple and complex. Simple types are defined as a set of attributes that define its behavior. First you have the name, which is required, and then a class that indicates where it is implemented. An example of a simple type is string, which is defined as:

```
<fieldType name="string" class="solr.StrField" sortMissingLast="true" />
```

Figure 52: Type definition

Complex types, besides storing data, include tokenizers and filters grouped into analyzers for additional processing. Let's define what each one is used for:

Tokenizer

Tokenizers are responsible for dividing the contents of a field into tokens. Wikipedia defines a token as: "a string of one or more characters that are significant as a group. The process of forming tokens from an input stream of characters is called tokenization." A token can be a letter, one word, or multiple words all embedded within a single phrase. How those tokens emerge depends on the tokenizer we are currently using.

For example, the Standard Tokenizer splits the text field into tokens, treating whitespace and punctuation as delimiters. Delimiter characters are discarded, with a couple of exceptions. Another example is the Lower Case Tokenizer that tokenizes the input stream by delimiting at non-letters and then converting all letters to lowercase. Whitespace and non-letters are discarded. A third one is the Letter Tokenizer, which creates tokens from strings of contiguous letters, discarding all non-letter characters. And the list goes on and on.

Filter

A filter consumes input and produces a stream of tokens. It basically looks at each token in the stream sequentially and decides whether to pass it along, replace it, or discard it. It can also do more complex analysis by looking ahead and considering multiple tokens at once, even though this is not very common.

Filters are chained; therefore, the order affects the outcome significantly. In a typical scenario, general filters are used first, while specialized ones are left at the end of the chain.

Analyzers

Field analyzers are in charge of examining the text of fields and producing an output stream. In simpler terms, they are a logical group of multiple operations made up of at least one (but potentially multiple) tokenizers and filters. It is possible to specify which analyzer should be used at query time or at index time.

```
<analyzer type="index">
<analyzer type="query">
```

Figure 53: Analyzers

Back to Complex Types

Let's take a look at one example. In this case, we are going to use one of the most commonly used types, `text_general`. By using this field to store text, you will be removing stop words and applying synonyms at query time, as well as other operations. Also, you can see that there are two analyzers: one for query time, and the other for index time.

```
<!-- A general text field that has reasonable, generic
     cross-language defaults: it tokenizes with StandardTokenizer,
  removes stop words from case-insensitive "stopwords.txt"
  (empty by default), and down cases.  At query time only, it
  also applies synonyms. -->
<fieldType name="text_general" class="solr.TextField" positionIncrementGap="100">
  <analyzer type="index">
    <tokenizer class="solr.StandardTokenizerFactory"/>
    <filter class="solr.StopFilterFactory" ignoreCase="true" words=
    "stopwords.txt" />
    <!-- in this example, we will only use synonyms at query time
    <filter class="solr.SynonymFilterFactory" synonyms="index_synonyms.txt"
    ignoreCase="true" expand="false"/>
    -->
    <filter class="solr.LowerCaseFilterFactory"/>
  </analyzer>
  <analyzer type="query">
    <tokenizer class="solr.StandardTokenizerFactory"/>
    <filter class="solr.StopFilterFactory" ignoreCase="true" words=
    "stopwords.txt" />
    <filter class="solr.SynonymFilterFactory" synonyms="synonyms.txt" ignoreCase
    ="true" expand="true"/>
    <filter class="solr.LowerCaseFilterFactory"/>
  </analyzer>
</fieldType>
```

Figure 54: Text general type

Field Definitions

In this section, you specify which fields will make up your index. For example, if you wanted to index and search over the books in Syncfusion's *Succinctly* Series or Pluralsight's Online trainings, then you could specify the following fields:

```
<field name="title" type="text_general" indexed="true" stored="true" multiValued="true"/>
<field name="subject" type="text_general" indexed="true" stored="true"/>
<field name="description" type="text_general" indexed="true" stored="true"/>
<field name="comments" type="text_general" indexed="true" stored="true"/>
<field name="author" type="text_general" indexed="true" stored="true"/>
<field name="keywords" type="text_general" indexed="true" stored="true"/>
<field name="category" type="text_general" indexed="true" stored="true"/>
```

Figure 55: Solr fields for sample data

A field definition has a name, a type, and multiple attributes that tell Solr how to manage each specific field. These are known as Static Fields.

Solr first looks for static definitions, and if none are found, it tries to find a match in dynamic fields. Dynamic fields are not covered in this book.

Copy Fields

You might want to interpret some document fields in more than one way. For this purpose, Solr has a way of performing automatic field copying. To do this, you specify in `copyField` tag the source, description, and optionally, a max size as `maxChars` of the field you wish to copy. Multiple fields can easily be copied into a single `copyField` using this functionality.

```
<copyField source="cat" dest="text"/>
<copyField source="name" dest="text"/>
<copyField source="manu" dest="text"/>
<copyField source="features" dest="text"/>
<copyField source="includes" dest="text"/>
<copyField source="manu" dest="manu_exact"/>
```

Figure 56: Solr copy fields

Copy fields can also be specified using patterns; for example, *source="*_i"* will copy all fields that end in _*i* to a single `copyField`.

Field Properties by Use Case

In the Apache Solr documentation wiki, there is an incredibly useful table that tells you the required values of the attributes for each use case. I am copying the table here verbatim, and will explain with an example. Please look for "Field Properties by Use Case" in the Solr wiki for more information.

Use Case	indexed	stored	multiValued	omitNorms	termVectors	termPositions	docValues
Search within field	TRUE						
Retrieve contents		TRUE					
Use as unique key	TRUE		FALSE				
Sort on field	TRUE		FALSE	TRUE			TRUE
Use field boosts				FALSE			
Document boosts affect searches within field				FALSE			
Highlighting	TRUE	TRUE			TRUE	TRUE	
Faceting	TRUE						TRUE
Add multiple values, maintaining order			TRUE				
Field length affects doc score				FALSE			
MoreLikeThis					TRUE		

Figure 57: Field properties by use case

The way to use this table is to look for the specific scenario that you want for your field, and determine the attributes. Let's say you want a field where you can search, sort, and retrieve contents.

This means there are three scenarios: *Search within field*, *Retrieve contents,* and *Sort on field*. Looking for the required attributes in the columns, you would need to set *indexed="true"*, *stored="true"*, and *multivalued="false"*.

Common Mistakes with Schema.Xml

Now let's talk about how to avoid some of the mistakes that people make with the schema.xml.

1. You need to keep your schema.xml simple and organized. I actually have a friend that cleans up the entire schema.xml first, then adds the sections that she needs. I think you may not actually need to go to that extent, but everybody has their own way of working.

2. There's the other extreme where some people just change the field names from the default configuration. I say this could bring some unintended consequences, as you will be copying the fields into other fields that you don't actually intend to.

3. And then there's another extreme, where there are some people who do a lot of over-planning and have the "everything but the kitchen sink" methodology. They over-plan for things that they don't even intend to use. There is an acronym that describes this very well: YAGNI, or, "you aren't gonna need it." Planning is good, but over-planning is usually bad. Don't include attributes and fields that you don't need.

4. Finally, this may not be a mistake, but it's a good recommendation: upgrade your Solr when possible. Solr has a very active development community, and you should upgrade when there are new versions available. Of course, stick to what works with your development capacity.

Succinctly Schema.Xml

It's time to make it our own Solr with our data. We will take our sample data, which can be found in GitHub in the following repository: https://github.com/xaviermorera/solr-succinctly.git.

Figure 58: The exercise repository

The repository includes two main folders:

- The source files for the exercises, located in the **assets** folder. It is under 50KB in size, so you can download them separately if required.

- A finished example, which you may not need if you follow the instructions provided in this book.

Understanding the documents that we will index in this demo is easy. In the real world, it can be trickier.

Create Your Collection

Up until now, we indexed some sample documents included in the Solr download. We will use this collection as a base to create our own, and will use a more appropriate name. It is worth mentioning that whenever the word "document" is used, it refers to a logical group of data. It is basically like saying a "record" or "row" in database language. I've been in meetings where non-search-savvy attendees only think of Word documents (or something similar) when we use this specific word. Don't get confused.

Here are the steps to create our first index:

- Open the command line and navigate to where we unzipped Solr earlier. It should be in *C:\solr-succinctly\succinctly\solr*. This is where collection1 is located.
- In this directory, you will find the collections that are available in the current installation. Right now, we only have collection1. We need to clone collection1, so please copy and paste, and rename the new collection to **succinctlybooks**.

Name	Date modified	Type	Size
bin	9/8/2014 3:56 AM	File folder	
collection1	12/13/2014 8:01 PM	File folder	
succinctlybooks	12/26/2014 3:26 PM	File folder	
README.txt	10/26/2014 5:57 AM	Text Document	3 KB
solr.xml	10/26/2014 5:57 AM	XML Document	2 KB
zoo.cfg	10/26/2014 5:57 AM	CFG File	1 KB

Figure 59: Create succinctlybooks collection

Now go into the succinctlybooks folder and open `core.properties`. Here is where you specify the name of the core, which is also called collection. It should look like this:

Figure 60: Name the collection

Now restart your Solr and go to the Core Selector. Succinctlybooks should be displayed.

Figure 61: New collection loaded

If you forget to rename the collection name within `core.properties` and try to restart, you will get an error telling you that the collection already exists. The error displayed in the console will be similar to the following:

```
2972 [main] ERROR org.apache.solr.core.SolrCore
ull:org.apache.solr.common.SolrException: Found multiple cores with the
name [collection1], with instancedirs [C:\solr-
succinctly\succinctly\solr\collection1\] and [C:\solr-
succinctly\succinctly\solr\succinctlybooks\]
```

Quick Cleanup

It is not a requirement to clear the index and comment out the existing fields; however, given that we have data in our index, we need to do it to avoid errors on fields we remove and types we change.

The following two steps will show you how to ensure we clean out the redundant data.

Step 1: Clear the index

The collection that we just copied came with the sample data we indexed recently. So where does Solr store the index data? Inside the current collection in a folder called "index" in the *data* folder. If you ever forget, just open the *Overview* section in the *Admin UI* section where you can see the current working directory (CWD), instance location, data, and index.

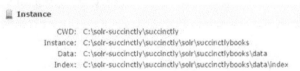

Figure 62: The index as seen in the Admin UI

In our case, it can be found here: *C:\solr-succinctly\succinctly\solr\succinctlybooks\data\index*. If you view the folder contents, this is what a Lucene index looks like:

Name	Date modified	Type	Size
_0.fdt	12/17/2014 11:37...	FDT File	5 KB
_0.fdx	12/17/2014 11:37...	FDX File	1 KB
_0.fnm	12/17/2014 11:37...	FNM File	3 KB
_0.nvd	12/17/2014 11:37...	NVD File	1 KB
_0.nvm	12/17/2014 11:37...	NVM File	1 KB
_0.si	12/17/2014 11:37...	SI File	1 KB
_0.tvd	12/17/2014 11:37...	TVD File	1 KB
_0.tvx	12/17/2014 11:37...	TVX File	1 KB
_0_Lucene41_0.doc	12/17/2014 11:37...	Microsoft Word 9...	2 KB
_0_Lucene41_0.pay	12/17/2014 11:37...	PAY File	1 KB
_0_Lucene41_0.pos	12/17/2014 11:37...	POS File	3 KB
_0_Lucene41_0.tim	12/17/2014 11:37...	TIM File	15 KB
_0_Lucene41_0.tip	12/17/2014 11:37...	TIP File	1 KB
segments.gen	12/17/2014 11:37...	GEN File	1 KB
segments_2	12/17/2014 11:39...	File	1 KB
write.lock	12/13/2014 8:01 PM	LOCK File	0 KB

Figure 63: A Lucene index

The next step is to clear the index, as we will be modifying the fields so that we can create our new index. Please stop Solr first by typing **Ctrl + C** from the console window where you started Solr, open Windows Explorer in your Lucene index, select all files within the index, and delete.

When you restart Solr, your index now has 0 documents. We now have an empty index to start with.

It is necessary to point out that if you do not delete the index, we will be changing the `uniquekey` from `string` to `int`. Given that some of the keys in the original samples have keys that look like "MA147LL/A," you will get the following error when you restart:

SolrCore Initialization Failures

succinctlybooks: org.apache.solr.common.SolrException:org.apache.solr.common.SolrException: Error Initializing QueryElevationComponent.

Please check your logs for more information

Figure 64: A Solr error

Soon, we will be changing our uniquekey's name, but not its type. If you insist that you want `int` as the type for `bookid` instead of `string`, you will get the error I just showed you at the start, even if you have a clean index. Figure 65 shows the error you will run into if you do not follow the instructions.

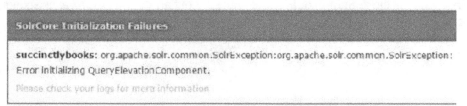
```
Caused by: org.apache.solr.common.SolrException: Invalid Number: MA147LL/A
    at org.apache.solr.schema.TrieField.readableToIndexed(TrieField.java:489)
    at org.apache.solr.schema.TrieField.readableToIndexed(TrieField.java:379)
    at org.apache.solr.handler.component.QueryElevationComponent$ElevationObj.<init>(QueryElevationComponent.java:191)
    at org.apache.solr.handler.component.QueryElevationComponent.loadElevationMap(QueryElevationComponent.java:324)
    at org.apache.solr.handler.component.QueryElevationComponent.inform(QueryElevationComponent.java:238)
    ... 10 more
```

Figure 65: A Solr error stack trace

I'll leave it to you to play around and figure out what the **`elevate.xml`** file is used for, which is one of the two potential culprits of this error:

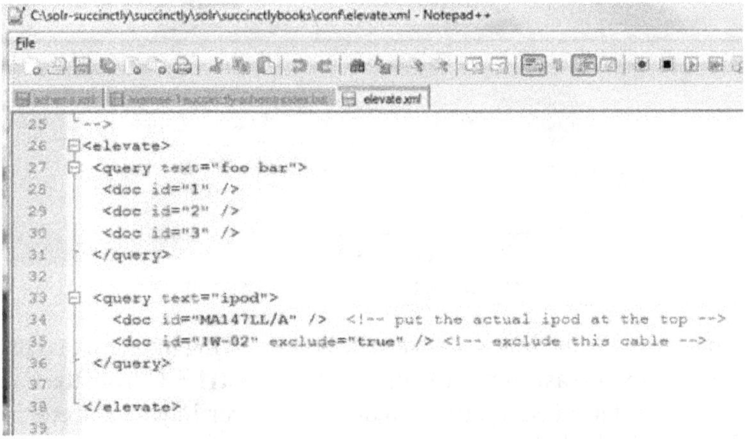

Figure 66: Elevate.xml

Step 2: Comment out existing fields

There are two sections that I like to remove within Schema.xml:

- The field definitions for the out-of-the-box sample data.
- Solr Cell fields.

First, look for the definition of *id* and comment it out all the way to *store,* as shown in the following image. Do it with an XML comment, which starts with `<!--` and ends in `-->`.

```
<!-- Commented out as part of Succinctly Solr Schema.Xml Excercise
   <field name="id" type="string" indexed="true" stored="true" required="true" multiValued="false" />

   <field name="sku" type="text_en_splitting_tight" indexed="true" stored="true" omitNorms="true"/>
   <field name="name" type="text_general" indexed="true" stored="true"/>
   <field name="manu" type="text_general" indexed="true" stored="true" omitNorms="true"/>
   <field name="cat" type="string" indexed="true" stored="true" multiValued="true"/>
   <field name="features" type="text_general" indexed="true" stored="true" multiValued="true"/>
   <field name="includes" type="text_general" indexed="true" stored="true" termVectors="true" termPos

   <field name="weight" type="float" indexed="true" stored="true"/>
   <field name="price"  type="float" indexed="true" stored="true"/>
   <field name="popularity" type="int" indexed="true" stored="true" />
   <field name="inStock" type="boolean" indexed="true" stored="true" />

   <field name="store" type="location" indexed="true" stored="true"/>
-->
```

Figure 67: Commenting out existing fields

Now let's look for the Solr Cell fields, and comment out from title all the way to links. There are a few more fields that you should comment out, which are **`content`**, manu_exact, and `payloads`. Notice I did not comment out text, as it is a catchall field implemented via `copyFields`. We will soon get to it.

```
<!--
<field name="title" type="text_general" indexed="true" stored="true" multivalued="true"/>
<field name="subject" type="text_general" indexed="true" stored="true"/>
<field name="description" type="text_general" indexed="true" stored="true"/>
<field name="comments" type="text_general" indexed="true" stored="true"/>
<field name="author" type="text_general" indexed="true" stored="true"/>
```
Figure 68: Solr Cell fields

Finally, look for `copyFields` and comment them out.

```
<!--copyField source="cat" dest="text"/>
<copyField source="name" dest="text"/>
<copyField source="manu" dest="text"/>
<copyField source="features" dest="text"/>
<copyField source="includes" dest="text"/>
<copyField source="manu" dest="manu_exact"/-->

<!-- Copy the price into a currency enabled field (default USD) -->
<!--copyField source="price" dest="price_c"/-->

<!-- Text fields from SolrCell to search by default in our catch-all field -->
<!--copyField source="title" dest="text"/>
<copyField source="author" dest="text"/>
<copyField source="description" dest="text"/>
<copyField source="keywords" dest="text"/>
<copyField source="content" dest="text"/>
<copyField source="content_type" dest="text"/>
<copyField source="resourcename" dest="text"/>
<copyField source="url" dest="text"/-->

<!-- Create a string version of author for faceting -->
<!--copyField source="author" dest="author_s"/-->
```
Figure 69: copyFields commented out

Leave `dynamicFields` and `uniqueKey` as they are; we will get to them soon.

Start by Understanding Your Data

Creating a search UI for Syncfusion's *Succinctly* series could take a long time, and potentially give you some headaches—or it can be done rather quickly, if you have the proper resources. And if you have this book in your hands, you are in luck, as you have a proper resource. Here is the data that we will be using:

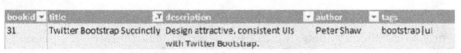

bookid	title	description	author	tags
31	Twitter Bootstrap Succinctly	Design attractive, consistent UIs with Twitter Bootstrap.	Peter Shaw	bootstrap|ui

Figure 70: Row of source data

- Bookid: The book id is just a number that will serve its purpose as a unique key.
- Title: The title of the book. This is the text that will be searched, stored, and retrieved.

- Description: A slightly larger text, with the description of the book.
- Author: The *Succinctly* series usually includes only one author per book; however, it is potentially multivalued, so we will declare as such. We will use this one as a facet.
- Tags: Another multivalued field; we'll use it also as a facet.

Open the **schema.xml** file for the "succinctlybooks" collection in Notepad++ or any other text editor. In case you forgot or skipped the previous exercises, it is located here: **C:\solr-succinctly\succinctly\solr\succinctlybooks\conf**.

It is time to define our static fields. The fields should be located in the same section as the sample data fields that we just commented out. Please look for the *id* field definition, and add them at the same level, starting with bookid.

Bookid will be our unique key. We declare a field with this name, and add the type, which in this case is string. If you want, it can also be an int; it does not really make a big difference. Given that it is a uniquekey, it needs to be indexed to retrieve a specific document; it is required, and unique keys cannot be multivalued. Remember **Field Properties by Use Case**? Also, please be mindful of capitalization; for example, multiValued has an upper-case V.

```
<field name="bookid" type="string" indexed="true"
stored="true" required="true" multiValued="false" />
```

Figure 71: Bookid

We changed the name of the unique key from id to bookid. Look for the uniquekey tag and change accordingly.

```
<uniqueKey>bookid</uniqueKey>
```

Figure 72: Unique key changed

And now we define the rest of the static fields. You should end up with some entries in the schema like this:

```
<field name="title" type="text_general" indexed="true" stored="true"/>
<field name="description" type="text_general" indexed="true" stored="true"/>
<field name="author" type="string" indexed="true" stored="true"/>
<field name="tags" type="string" indexed="true" stored="true" multiValued="true"/>
```

Figure 73: Schema entries

You may have noticed by now that *title* and *description* are of type text_general, while author and tags are of type string. As you might have guessed, these are different data types in the Solr landscape.

String is defined as a simple type with no tokenization. That is, it stores a word or sentence as an exact string, as there are no analyzers. It is useful for exact matches, i.e. for faceting.

```
<fieldType name="string" class="solr.StrField" sortMissingLast="true" />
```

Figure 74: String definition

On the other hand, the type definition of *text_*general is more complex, including *query* and *index* time analyzers, for performing tokenization and secondary processing like lower casing. It's useful for all scenarios when we want to match part of a sentence. If you define title as a string, and then you searched for *jquery,* you would not find *jQuery Succinctly.* You would need to query for the exact string. This is not what we would most definitively want.

```
<fieldType name="text_general" class="solr.TextField" positionIncrementGap="100">
  <analyzer type="index">
    <tokenizer class="solr.StandardTokenizerFactory"/>
    <filter class="solr.StopFilterFactory" ignoreCase="true" words="stopwords.txt" />
    <!-- in this example, we will only use synonyms at query time
    <filter class="solr.SynonymFilterFactory" synonyms="index_synonyms.txt" ignoreCase="true" expand="false"/>
    -->
    <filter class="solr.LowerCaseFilterFactory"/>
  </analyzer>
  <analyzer type="query">
    <tokenizer class="solr.StandardTokenizerFactory"/>
    <filter class="solr.StopFilterFactory" ignoreCase="true" words="stopwords.txt" />
    <filter class="solr.SynonymFilterFactory" synonyms="synonyms.txt" ignoreCase="true" expand="true"/>
    <filter class="solr.LowerCaseFilterFactory"/>
  </analyzer>
</fieldType>
```

Figure 75: Querying the string

We will be creating facets for tags and authors, which means a string is the correct type to use for these. Will we be able to find them if we only type the name or last name? Let's wait and see.

Summary

In this chapter, we started looking at the schema.xml file. We found out how important this file is to Solr, and we started editing it to define our own collection containing information about the *Succinctly* e-book series.

In the next chapter, we'll move on to the next stage in our game plan and cover the subject of indexing.

Chapter 6 Indexing

Making Your Content Searchable

When you hear the word "indexing" in the context of Solr—or other search engines for that matter—it basically means taking content, tokenizing it, modifying it if necessary, adding it to the index, and then making it searchable. Solr retrieves results very fast because it searches an inverted index, instead of searching text directly.

But what exactly is an inverted index? It is a data structure that stores a mapping from content, like words or numbers, to its location in a set of documents. Because of this, searching becomes very fast, as the price is paid at indexing time instead of at query time. Another way of referring to an inverted index is as a postings file or inverted file. So if you hear any of these three terms, they mean the same thing.

During indexing, Solr inverts a page-centric data structure to a keyword-centric data structure. A word can be found in many pages. Solr stores this index in a directory called *index* in the *data* directory. There are many ways of indexing your content; in this chapter, I'll introduce you to a couple of them.

Indexing is nothing new—humanity has been doing it for centuries! This is something that we do all the time in our busy lives. The index at the back of a book for example, or a TV guide telling you which programs are on your TV stations, are both perfect examples of indexing in action.

You use them by quickly scanning a predefined list, looking for some meaningful keyword or topic. Once the keyword or topic is found, the entry will contain some kind of a pointer (for example, a page number) that allows you to go straight to the information you seek.

Indexing Techniques

We've already indexed some data using the `post.jar` tool, but there are many more options:

- You can use the Solr cell framework built on Apache Tika for binary files, like PDF, Word, Excel, and more.
- It is also possible to upload XML files by sending them via HTTP requests.
- The `DataImportHandler` allows accessing a database to retrieve data, but it is not limited to databases. The `DataImportHandler` can also read from RSS feeds or many other data sources.
- You can also build your custom Java application via Solr's Java client API, SolrJ.
- And for those of you who love .NET like I do, you have SolrNet.
- As I mentioned before, there are other content processing pipeline tools like the Search Technologies ASPIRE post-to-Solr tool.
- And finally, you can build your own on top of Solr's RESTful interface.

Indexing the *Succinctly* Series

In this section, we will play around with data by indexing, updating, and deleting. The focus here is to do things in a few different ways so that you can improve your skills.

Here is what we will do:

- Start by indexing using CSV and the post.jar tool.
- Then, learn how to update documents using the Admin UI.
- Next, we go into how to delete documents.
- Next, we'll cover the Solr XML format.
- Finally, we'll be indexing with two useful tools, cURL and Fiddler.

Indexing Documents Using CSV

Indexing documents is very easy if you have structured and properly escaped CSV files of your data. We've already defined the static fields in our Schema.xml, so next we need to get our data imported.

Start by opening the assets folder in our samples located in GitHub. Please review the repository you have cloned and confirm it looks like the following:

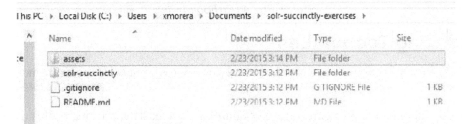

Figure 77: GitHub repository

Now from the assets folder, using Windows Explorer, please copy **exercise-1-succinctly-schema.csv** and **exercise-1-succinctly-schema.csv** to our **exampledocs** folder in **C:\solr-succinctly\succinctly\exampledocs**.

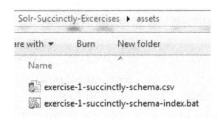

Figure 78: Exercise 1

You might be wondering why we are copying the CSV and BAT files to `exampledocs`. This is because that is where `post.jar` is located, and even though you can set the correct paths, it is easier this way.

The next step is to execute index the files. For this purpose, we will open a command prompt and navigate to the `exampledocs` folder. You can just run the `exercise-1-succinctly-schema.bat` file, which will execute the following command:

```
java -Durl=http://localhost:8983/solr/succinctlybooks/update -
Dtype=text/csv -jar post.jar "exercise-1-succinctly-schema.csv"
```

Read the response in the command window. If all went well, it will prompt "1 files indexed."

```
C:\Windows\system32\cmd.exe

C:\solr-succinctly\succinctly\exampledocs>exercise-1-succinctly-schema-index.bat

C:\solr-succinctly\succinctly\exampledocs>java -Durl=http://localhost:8983/solr/succi
ema.csv"
SimplePostTool version 1.5
Posting files to base url http://localhost:8983/solr/succinctlybooks/update using con
POSTing file exercise-1-succinctly-schema.csv
1 Files indexed.
COMMITting Solr index changes to http://localhost:8983/solr/succinctlybooks/update..
Time spent: 0:00:00.513
```

Figure 79: Sample file indexed

Excellent! Let's run a query now in `succinctlybooks` for *:*. You can do it from the

Admin UI.

If you do not get this response, please make sure that the exercise files are within the `exampledocs` folder, right next to `post.jar`. Also, run `post.jar /?` from `exampledocs` to confirm that it is able to execute.

Figure 80: Query with all books

Everything looks great. We have 50 documents and our data seems ok. Let's analyze one record:

```
{
  "bookid": "2",
  "title": "Git Succinctly",
  "description": "Get up and running with one of the fastest spreading revision control systems out there.",
  "author": "Ryan Hodson",
  "tags": [
    "git|source-control"
  ],
  "_version_": 1488703960134975500
},
```

Figure 81: Single record

Something doesn't look right. Can you pinpoint what it is? Look at `tags`. You probably noticed by now, but let's make it a bit more obvious. Within tags, there is only one entry with "git|source-control". It is a multivalued field, but it is treating `git` and `source-control` as part of the same tag. For this example to be correct, they should be two separate values.

To review further, please click the link below for the response, with xml as wt (response writer):

```
http://localhost:8983/solr/succinctlybooks/select?
q=*%3A*&wt=xml&indent=true
```

 Note: If you have modified Solr's location, please use your current location.

Let's look at the same record for *Git Succinctly*.

```
▼<doc>
    <str name="bookid">2</str>
    <str name="title">Git Succinctly</str>
  ▼<str name="description">
      Get up and running with one of the fastest-spreading revision control systems out there.
    </str>
    <str name="author">Ryan Hodson</str>
  ▼<arr name="tags">
      <str>git|source-control</str>
    </arr>
    <long name="_version_">1488703960134975488</long>
  </doc>
```

Figure 82: Document with error on tags

You should be able to see from the previous figure that the tags field has been indexed as a single field, not multiple fields, even though we declared as multivalued. The reason this happened is very simple: we did not tell post.jar which field we want to separate, and which one is the separator.

We can easily fix this by running the following command:

```
java -Durl="http://localhost:8983/solr/succinctlybooks/update?
f.tags.split=true&f.tags.separator=|" -Dtype=text/csv -jar post.jar
"exercise-1-succinctly-schema.csv"
```

I've also included the fix in the following file in our assets folder: `exercise-1-succinctly-schema-index-fixseparator.bat`.

Once we've made this change, try re-running the previous queries; you should see a difference.

```
▼<doc>
    <str name="bookid">2</str>
    <str name="title">Git Succinctly</str>
  ▼<str name="description">
      Get up and running with one of the fastest-spreading revision control systems out there.
    </str>
    <str name="author">Ryan Hodson</str>
  ▼<arr name="tags">
      <str>git</str>
      <str>source-control</str>
    </arr>
    <long name="_version_">1488704766529765376</long>
  </doc>
```

Figure 83: Correct multivalue tags

Whenever you have to specify multivalue inputs as a single string, you must ensure that you tell Solr it needs to split the input up, using the following parameter:

```
f.tag.encapsulator='<separator character here>'
```

Indexing via Admin UI

You can also create and amend indexes using the Admin UI in the Documents section. For our first example, let's prove that the record that I am about to add does not already exist. Open the Core Selector, click on **Query**, and in the q input field, type in bookid:51 and execute the query. No documents found. We will add book number 51, which is this one you are reading right now.

```
{
  "responseHeader": {
    "status": 0,
    "QTime": 1,
    "params": {
      "indent": "true",
      "q": "bookid:51",
      "_": "1419740373786",
      "wt": "json"
    }
  },
  "response": {
    "numFound": 0,
    "start": 0,
    "docs": []
  }
}
```

Figure 84: No book with ID 51

Now select **Documents** and type in the following text within Document(s) input field:

```
{"bookid":"51","title":"Solr Succinctly","description":"Solr Succinctly
gets you started in the enterprise search world.","author":"Xavier
Morera","tags":"enterprise-search"}
```

Click **Submit Document**, and you should get a success status in the right-hand section. Leave this window open, as we will use it in the upcoming two sections, and open a new tab in the same location to continue testing.

Request-Handler (qt)

/update

Document Type

JSON

Document(s)

{"bookid":"51","title":"Solr Succinctly","description":"Solr Succinctly gets you started in the enterprise search world.","author":"Xavier Morera","tags":"enterprise-search"}

Status: success
Response:
```
{
  "responseHeader": {
    "status": 0,
    "QTime": 4
  }
}
```

Figure 85: Document submitted

Now the book is available in the index, and is searchable.

Figure 86: Book with ID 51 available

If you were to try and run this as a singular query all on its own as follows:

```
http://localhost:8983/solr/succinctlybooks/select?
q=Solr&wt=xml&indent=true
```

You may be surprised to find that you don't get any results. I'll leave the explanation to this until a little bit later; for now, I want to show you a little more about how Solr searches its indexes.

Updating via Admin UI

We just added one document. But what if we wanted to update a document? It's very simple—you just add the document again. Remove my last name and leave `"author":"Xavier"`. Click **Submit Document** and the run the query again. You will see that my name has been updated, sans last name.

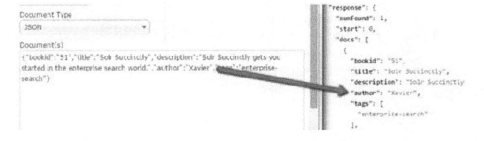

Figure 87: Author modified

If you look just below the document input field, you'll see an input parameter called `Overwrite`; initially this will be set to `true`. Its purpose with this default setting is to ensure that it updates where needed and doesn't insert a new record. Set it to `false`, and try changing the author name again, and you should find that it now adds a new record instead:

Figure 88: Overwrite option

Partial Updates

Partial updates is a feature people have been requesting for years in Solr; however, it was not until Solr 4.0 that it became available. Put simply, partial updating involves updating a single field within a document without the need for indexing the full document. This may not sound like much, but if you have big documents (and a lot of them) that require a huge amount of processing just for a simple single field change, you can quickly see how much processing time would be wasted. This along with the sheer number of documents can make a big difference.

Let me share with you a story that happened to me a few years ago. I was working on a project for a patent searching application. It basically had a double digit TB index, made up of about 96MM patents containing every patent application and grant filed for all patent authorities worldwide. Document sizes ranged from a few bytes to many megabytes; we had thousands of fields, and indexing a document meant consuming a lot of processing power due to field normalization and many other required operations.

Each patent entry has one or many classification codes that basically specify the content of each patent; these codes used USPC, ECLA, and many others, depending on the owning authority.

From January 1, 2013 on, the Cooperative Patent Classification started to use as the official new classification, a scheme jointly developed by the United States Patent and Trademark Office and the European Patent Office.

This meant that all patents suddenly needed to be reclassified, the upshot of which was basically to add a new field for the new CPC classification code. In technical terms, this wasn't a huge task by any stretch of the imagination. We received a CSV file that contained the patent canonical number and the CPC codes, so we knew exactly what needed to be matched to which records. All patents needed to be searchable with the new CPC code, and this is where our problems began. We did not have the ability to perform partial updates, meaning we had to fully reprocess about 80 million+ documents for every single update—a task that took weeks to do.

A partial update could've reduced the amount of time needed to a couple of days. The moral of the story is simple: use partial updates where possible, and you'll quickly realize how invaluable they are.

Let's do a partial update now. If you recall, here is what we have to index my book document:

```
{"bookid":"51","title":"Solr Succinctly","description":"Solr Succinctly
gets you started in the enterprise search world.","author":"Xavier
Morera","tags":"enterprise-search"}
```

Leave only `bookid` and `author`, changing `author` to Xavier Partial Update, and click **Submit Document**.

```
{"bookid":"51","author":"Xavier MT"}
```

Now run the query to retrieve this document. What happened? Basically, when you did the update, it added the full record with the fields you specified. Full update is not what we need; we need partial update.

```
"response": {
  "numFound": 1,
  "start": 0,
  "docs": [
    {
      "bookid": "51",
      "author": "Xavier MT",
      "_version_": 1488709702733791200
    }
```

Figure 89: Full update

Let's try again. Start by resetting the document to its original state. Run the query to confirm.

```
{"bookid":"51","title":"Solr Succinctly","description":"Solr Succinctly
gets you started in the enterprise search world.","author":"Xavier
Morera","tags":"enterprise-search"}
```

Once you reset things, try to submit a partial update again. Specify which field you want to update by using the key word `set` within {}, as follows:

```
{"bookid":"51","author":{"set":"Xavier MT"}}
```

Run the query again for `bookid`. Now you will have a partial update on `author`.

```
"response": {
 "numFound": 1,
 "start": 0,
 "docs": [
   {
     "bookid": "51",
     "title": "Solr Succinctly",
     "description": "Solr Succinctly gets you started in the enterprise search world.",
     "author": "Xavier MT",
     "tags": [
       "enterprise-search"
     ],
     " version ": 1488709961884106800
   }
```

Figure 90: Partial update

One last thing you need to be aware of: for a partial update to work correctly, you must have all your fields set to `stored=true`. This can be an issue if you wanted to manage your index size by not having all fields stored, but if not specified, you won't be able to do a partial update on that field.

Deleting Data

Now that we know how to insert and update documents, the next step is to learn how to delete documents. You can delete documents by ID and by Query. For example, to delete this book from the index, you could use either of the two following ways:

The first is to delete by ID. This is the command that will tell Solr which ID it needs to delete:

```
<delete>
<id>51</id>
</delete>
```

The URL that you should use to execute this is as follows:

http://localhost:8983/solr/succinctlybooks/update?stream.body=<delete>
<id>51</id></delete>&commit=true

The response obtained should look like the following. A status of o means no errors were returned.

```
▼<response>
 ▼<lst name="responseHeader">
    <int name="status">0</int>
    <int name="QTime">36</int>
  </lst>
 </response>
```

Figure 91: Document deleted

However, it does not indicate the number of records, or if records were actually deleted. For this purpose, you would need to run a query to confirm. From the Admin UI, please select the `succinctlybooks` core, click on the `Query` section, add in *q* the following `bookid:51`, and execute.

```
{
  "responseHeader": {
    "status": 0,
    "QTime": 1,
    "params": {
      "indent": "true",
      "q": "bookid:51",
      "_": "1419806754186",
      "wt": "json"
    }
  },
  "response": {
    "numFound": 0,
    "start": 0,
    "docs": []
  }
}
```

Figure 92: Query to confirm record deleted

To delete by query, you can try the following command:

```
<delete>
<query>author:"Xavier Morera"</query>
</delete>
```

The URL to execute it is as follows:

```
http://localhost:8983/solr/succinctlybooks/update?
stream.body=%3Cdelete%3E%3Cquery%3Eauthor:%22Xavier%20Morera%22%3C/query%3E
```

By this point, you should be able to see that it's possible to delete the entire index, simply by using the following URL:

```
http://localhost:8983/solr/succinctlybooks/update?stream.body=<delete>
<query>*:*</query></delete>&commit=true
```

Specifying a wildcard is way more efficient than specifying each index individually, something which is not always possible, as Solr may have files locked.

It is worth noting that you need to set `commit` to `true`, or else it won't be committed to the index. If you are deleting multiple documents, it is preferred if you don't do a commit on every single operation.

Also, you can delete documents that match multiple fields. Any query that you can build for searching can also be used for deleting. Then, if you're using SolrNet or SolrJ, you can do a call to their API using the function `solr.deleteByQuery`*:*. We will not be covering the API of SolrJ or SolrNet in this book, but I believe it is worth mentioning.

Solr XML Format

Solr has its own XML format, which is very specific and verbose, yet easy to read. It deals better with multi-valued optional fields, complex strings, and real-life requirements. I've participated in multiple projects where using Solr XML format is preferred, as document processing is done separately and potentially in parallel, generating millions of XML files that then are indexed in Solr as a separate process.

In the example files, you should find **exercise-2-solr-xml.xml**. If you open this file in a text editor, you should see that it basically has the **add** command, the document, and then all the fields that I'll be adding for this specific document. This book is not really in progress right now, but I just finished a course on it for Pluralsight, so it makes a good example subject.

```
1   <?xml version="1.0"?>
2   <!-- Solr Succinctly Test upload Solr XML -->
3   <add>
4     <doc>
5       <field name="bookid">52</field>
6       <field name="title">Kanban Succinctly</field>
7       <field name="description">Gets you started into the Kanban world in around 100 pages</field>
8       <field name="author">Xavier Moreras</field>
9       <field name="tags">kanban</field>
10      <field name="tags">agile</field>
11    </doc>
12  </add>
```

Figure 93: Indexing Solr XML sample data

Using one or both of the methods we learned earlier, perform a query for a book with an ID equal to 52; you can use the following URL, or enter it into the Admin UI query input:

```
http://localhost:8983/solr/succinctlybooks/select?
q=bookid%3A52&wt=json&indent=true
```

The next step is to add the document in the same way as we did with the CSV files. For ease of use, you'll find a batch file along with the XML; if you run this the document will be indexed.

exercise-2-solr-xml.bat	12/28/2014 5:19 PM	Windows Batch File
exercise-2-solr-xml.xml	12/28/2014 5:05 PM	XML Document

Figure 94: Copy sample files

If you're not on Windows, or cannot run batch files, then the command you need is as follows:

```
java -Dauto -Durl=http://localhost:8983/solr/succinctlybooks/update -jar
post.jar "exercise-2-solr-xml.xml"
```

Notice how I used –Dauto instead of specifying the file extension. The tool is able to process multiple extensions as depicted in the command line response.

```
C:\solr-succinctly\succinctly\exampledocs>exercise-2-solr-xml.bat

C:\solr-succinctly\succinctly\exampledocs>java -Dauto -Durl=http://localhost:8983/solr
SimplePostTool version 1.5
Posting files to base url http://localhost:8983/solr/succinctlybooks/update..
Entering auto mode. File endings considered are xml,json,csv,pdf,doc,docx,ppt,pptx,xls
POSTing file exercise-2-solr-xml.xml (text/xml)
1 files indexed.
COMMITing Solr index changes to http://localhost:8983/solr/succinctlybooks/update..
Time spent: 0:00:00.077
```

Figure 95: Index Solr XML file

Now run the query again for `bookid` 52. It will return one document.

```
{
  "responseHeader": {
    "status": 0,
    "QTime": 1,
    "params": {
      "indent": "true",
      "q": "bookid:52",
      "_": "1419809018965",
      "wt": "json"
    }
  },
  "response": {
    "numFound": 1,
    "start": 0,
    "docs": [
      {
        "bookid": "52",
        "title": "Kanban Succinctly",
        "description": "Gets you started into the Kanban world in around 100 pages",
        "author": "Xavier Morera",
        "tags": [
          "kanban",
          "agile"
        ],
        "_version_": 1488777528226087000
      }
    ]
  }
}
```

Figure 96: Query for bookid 52

If you get this far, give yourself a pat on the back—you're well on your way to understanding how Solr works and creating your own search indexes.

Using cURL

cURL is a command line tool for transferring data using various protocols, one which typically needs admin access in a shell-based scope, but is simple and easy to use. When it comes to working with Solr, I can say that cURL is your friend. It is great because it is easy to use, and you can easily post binary files. A training on cURL is beyond the scope of this book, but I will show you a quick demo of how it can be used. Also, if you are in an environment where you can't use cURL, you can achieve similar results using plugins like Chrome's Postman plugin.

To get started, you need to download cURL, which is very simple to install.

You actually use cURL from the command line. It allows you to post information and even post files. It lets you add, update, and delete documents.

To invoke it, type **cURL** in the command line, and then the location of your update handler. You also need to include which core you're actually committing it to.

Regarding parameters, I am passing `commit` equals `true`, which means the information should be committed to the index once I issue the command. Then I'm passing `-H` for the header, with a content type of `text/XML`.

Next is the command for the Solr. In this case, I'm doing an `add` command, which is exactly the same as in the Solr XML format, with the fields that I want included in this document.

The cURL command to complete all of these operations is as follows:

```
curl http://localhost:8983/solr/succinctlybooks/update?commit=true -H
"Content-Type: text/xml" --data-binary "<add><doc><field
name=\"bookid\">53</field><field name=\"title\">Scrum Succinctly</field>
<field name=\"author\">Xavier Morera</field><field
name=\"tags\">scrum</field></doc></add>"
```

To make your life easier, I have also included **exercise-3-curl.bat** to the **exampledocs** folder in **succinctlybooks** and run it. You must ensure that your system can find and run the cURL program for the batch file to work.

| exercise-3-curl.bat | 12/28/2014 5:45 PM | Windows Batch File |

Figure 97: Bat File for cURL Exercise

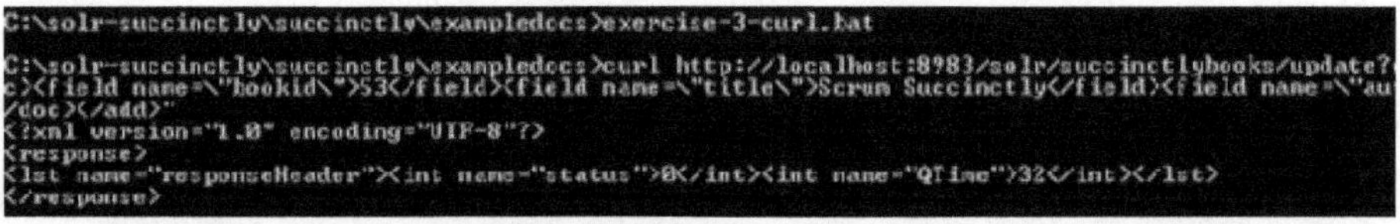

Figure 98: Indexed via cURL

You should be able to see that the status of the previous operation is `0`, which, as you now know, means no errors. If you subsequently run a query for a book with ID = 53, you should see one document appear within your results.

The document I indexed does not have all fields. Only `bookid` is required, but it is possible that if you copy pasted the field definitions and left `required="true"`, then Solr will prompt an exception message like this:

```
<str name="msg">[doc=53] missing required field: description</str>
```

If this scenario occurs, please make sure that only `bookid` contains a required="true" attribute within Schema.xml.

```
{
  "responseHeader": {
    "status": 0,
    "QTime": 1,
    "params": {
      "indent": "true",
      "q": "bookid:53",
      "_": "1419810363656",
      "wt": "json"
    }
  },
  "response": {
    "numFound": 1,
    "start": 0,
    "docs": [
      {
        "bookid": "53",
        "title": "Scrum Succinctly",
        "author": "Xavier Morera",
        "tags": [
          "scrum"
        ],
        "_version_": 1488779056108273700
      }
    ]
  }
}
```

Figure 99: Bookid 53

You can also issue any other command you wish. For example, a `delete` command would look like this:

```
curl http://localhost:8983/solr/succinctlybooks/update?commit=true -H
"Content-Type: text/xml" --data-binary "<delete><query>courseid:getting-
started-enterprise-search-apache-solr*:*</query></delete>"
```

Fiddler

If you are used to web development, you are probably aware of Fiddler. If not, then Fiddler is a debugging proxy that logs all HTTP traffic into your computer. It's an excellent tool if you have problems, or if you want to debug the requests as you are working with Solr. Use it to inspect, reissue, and compose requests. To get Fiddler, visit http://getfiddler.com.

Once it is installed, open Fiddler. It starts monitoring all traffic within your computer, so I recommend you set a filter so that it only picks up local requests. To do so:

- Go to **Filters**
- Select **Show only Intranet Hosts**
- Choose **No Host Filter**

Figure 100: Fiddler filter

Besides monitoring, Fiddler can also issue requests. Let's learn how to issue a request.

Go to the **Composer** tab. You have the option of specifying which verb you want to use, such as GET or POST. In this case, I'm going to do a POST to the update handler, specifically to the **succinctlybooks** core. This is the URL:

```
http://localhost:8983/solr/succinctlybooks/update?wt=json
```

The next step is to add the headers. Don't worry about the content length; Fiddler adds it automatically.

```
User-Agent: Fiddler
Content-Type: application/json
Host: localhost:8983
Content-Length: 241
```

And now add the body:

```
{"add":
    { "doc":{
        "bookid":"54",
        "title":"dotTrace Succinctly",
        "description":"dotTrace in around 100 pages",
        "author":"Xavier Morera",
        "tags":"profiling"
        },
    "boost":1.0,
    "overwrite":true,
    "commitWithin":100
    }
}
```

Your Composer tab should appear as shown in Figure 101. Click **Execute**.

Figure 101: Execute in Fiddler composer

As soon as the request is issued, Fiddler will log it in the left panel. `Result 200` means all went well. If this is your first time using Fiddler, make a mistake on purpose to see an HTTP 500 response.

214   200   HTTP   localhost:8983   /solr/succinctlybooks/update?wt=json

Figure 102: A Fiddler response

Now double-click on the request, and Fiddler will open the details.

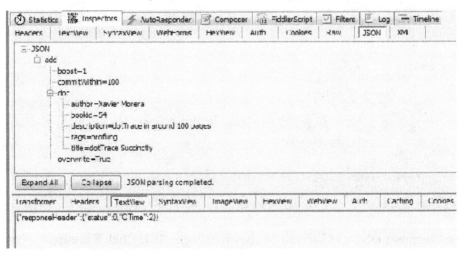

Figure 103: Response in Fiddler Inspector

You can also run queries:

#	Result	Protocol	Host	URL
144	200	HTTP	localhost:8983	/solr/succinctlybooks/select?q=bookid

Figure 104: Query Solr using Fiddler

You can then analyze the results:

Figure 105: Analyze a Solr response in Fiddler

As you can see, this is a very powerful tool.

Re-indexing in Solr

When you are running Solr in either your production or development environments, at some point you'll need to re-index. One scenario that requires re-indexing is when there is a schema change due to a new field being added. While it's true that you can make partial updates, there are some cases you need full updates, and performing a re-index is the only way to go.

Depending on the type of schema change, you may need to delete all your documents and then start re-indexing again from scratch. In this case, it's advantageous to have a full secondary set of Solr servers so you don't lose search capabilities while re-indexing takes place. The point is that while you are reindexing because of a schema change, you need to point your application to an exact copy of the original Solr index, and once reindexing is complete, you point your application to the new Solr index.

What exactly does re-indexing mean? Basically, it's the process of indexing every single document again, just as you did when you originally added them to the index.

In some cases, re-indexing can be painfully slow, because accessing the original data sources is not very efficient. If you run into a scenario like this, I suggest you set up an intermediate store, or another Solr that serves as a cache to help you re-index in a much quicker way.

Summary

In this chapter, you've learned how to index data, which is one of the most basic operations of Solr; it's how you insert data into the search engine. You learned how to index by using the included post.jar, a command line tool called cURL, and Fiddler. You also learned how to delete and update data. Regarding updates, we learned the difference between full and partial updates, a feature that not all search engines have.

And now it is time to learn how to configure Solr's core via Solrconfig.xml.

Chapter 7 SolrConfig.Xml

Configuring Solr

Solrconfig.xml is the main configuration file used to configure Solr's core. There are multiple sections that include XML statements used to set configuration values for a given collection, parameters which include important features like caching, event listeners, request handlers, request dispatchers, highlighter plugin configuration, data directory location, and items available in the admin UI section.

Request Handlers

One particularly important feature that can be configured is the request handler. A request handler is in charge of accepting an HTTP request, performing the search, and then returning the results back to the calling client.

Request handlers are specified using a QT parameter, and they define logic executed for any request passed to them.

You can, for example, include filters or facets. You can also make the changes in two modes. One way is to append, which adds them to the request without the user asking for them, or you can add an invariant. In this case, if you select invariant, it will be added to the request, and the user cannot modify it. Invariants are very useful for scoping or even for security.

Multiple request handlers can be specified in the same `solrconfig`, and you have named request handlers covering multiple Solr cores.

There are three types of query parameters in a request handler:

- **Defaults**: Provides default parameter values that will be used if a value specified at request time.

- **Appends**: Provides parameter values that will be used in addition to any values specified at request time or as defaults.

- **Invariants**: Provides parameter values that will be used in spite of any values provided at request time. It is a way of letting Solr lock down options available to Solr clients. Any parameters values specified here are used regardless of what values may be specified in either the query, the defaults, or the `appends` parameters.

The default request handler in a Solr installation is `/select`, which should by now be very familiar to you, as this is the one we've been using for each example so far in this book.

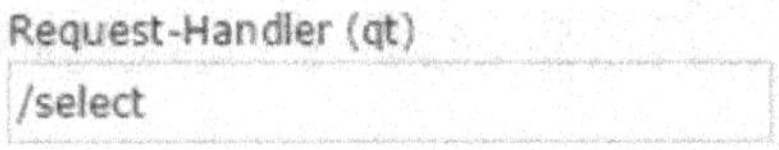

Figure 106: Default Request Handler as seen in the Admin UI

If you open your Solrconfig.Xml file and look for the handler, you will see that it basically has three defaults, the `echoParams`, `rows`, and `df` parameters. As previously mentioned, a requestHandler can have multiple other parameters defined to control how a query is handled via `appends` or `invariants`.

If I uncomment the included sample sections of the */select* request handler, we should see something that looks like the following:

```xml
<?xml version="1.0" encoding="UTF-8" ?>
<requestHandler name="/select" class="solr.SearchHandler">
  <lst name="defaults">
    <str name="echoParams">explicit</str>
    <int name="rows">10</int>
    <str name="df">text</str>
  </lst>
    <lst name="appends">
      <str name="fq">inStock:true</str>
    </lst>
    <lst name="invariants">
      <str name="facet.field">cat</str>
      <str name="facet.field">manu_exact</str>
      <str name="facet.query">price:[* TO 500]</str>
      <str name="facet.query">price:[500 TO *]</str>
    </lst>
    <arr name="components">
      <str>nameOfCustomComponent1</str>
      <str>nameOfCustomComponent2</str>
    </arr>
</requestHandler>
```

Figure 107: /select request handler

As you can see, this example is explicitly stating that any result to be returned has to be in stock. This is done by adding the filter query `instock:true`. Don't make these uncommenting changes yourself just yet; we're going to build our own handler in just a moment.

Creating a New Request Handler

Let's create a new request handler that only returns books for one specific author. This might not be a very realistic scenario, but it'll allow me to demonstrate how a handler works.

First, let's make sure that the handler does not exist. It's good practice to always perform this step just to make sure you haven't already defined a handler with that name. Pass the following URL to your Solr install using your browser:

```
http://localhost:8983/solr/succinctlybooks/books?
q=*%3A*&wt=json&indent=true
```

The following figure shows that you should receive a 404 error from that request; this is to be expected, and indicates that you are in fact safe to add the new handler.

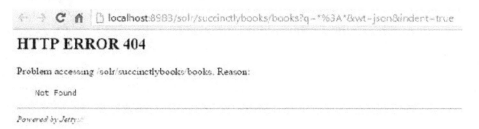

Figure 108: 404 error returned by Solr to show that the 'books' handler does not yet exist

Now open your **Solrconfig.Xml** located in your **solr/succinctlybooks/conf** folder. Please look for the **/select** request handler, copy it, and remove all commented out lines. Don't make any changes just yet. It should look something like this:

```
<requestHandler name="/books" class="solr.SearchHandler">
    <lst name="defaults">
        <str name="echoParams">explicit</str>
        <int name="rows">10</int>
        <str name="df">text</str>
    </lst>
</requestHandler>
```

Figure 109: Our new books handler

The next step is to navigate to the **Core Admin** and click **Reload**. By default, collection1 will be selected; please make sure you select **succinctlybooks**. Don't navigate away just yet—keep looking at the Reload button. It needs to turn green for a few seconds to indicate that reload was successful.

Figure 110: Reload Cores

Run the query again, but make sure you are using **/books** instead of the **/select** request handler, as shown in red:

```
http://localhost:8983/solr/succinctlybooks/books?
q=*%3A*&wt=json&indent=true
```

This time, it will most definitely work, and you have 53 results—the same 53 results. Let's make a couple of changes, starting with a very simple one.

Changing Rows in Request Handler

The number of results that you return to your users depends greatly on how you display your results. Some people do five results, others 10—I've seen applications that display 50. While this is different depending on the use case, setting it is easily done as follows.

Within Solrconfig.Xml, navigate to the `/books` request handler and change the rows parameter from `10` to `5`. Reload the **succinctlybooks** core and re-execute a *:* query.

 Tip: Every time you make a change to Solrconfig.xml it is required that you reload the core.

If we run the query before and after, we'll see that before we got 10 results, and afterwards we only get five:

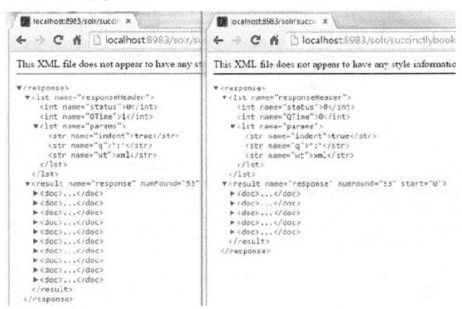

Figure 111: Compare change rows books handler

Ok, so this one was pretty easy. Let's do another one.

Appends in Request Handlers

The `/books` request handler returns all 53 documents—the 50 *Succinctly* series entries originally added, and the ones we added in the indexing chapter. Let's make a small change using an append so that all queries executed only return books that have my name as the author.

To do this, add an `appends` section where you specify a filter query for `author:"Xavier Morera"`. It should look something like Figure 111, showing the addition of an `'lst'` tag with a name of `'appends'` and an inner string tag with a name of `'fq'` specifying the filter.

```
<requestHandler name="/books" class="solr.SearchHandler">
    <lst name="defaults">
        <str name="echoParams">explicit</str>
        <int name="rows">5</int>
        <str name="df">text</str>
    </lst>
    <lst name="appends">
    <str name="fq">author:"Xavier Morera"</str>
    </lst>
</requestHandler>
```

Figure 112: /books handler appends section

Reload the core, and then run a query for all documents. You will get only three results.

Figure 113: Results with books handler appends

If you want a more specific query, try `q= description:you`. In this specific query, if you use `/select`, you will get two results. One of them is my book, and the other a book is by Cody Lindley.

Figure 114: Query results when the '/select' handler is used

If you do the same using our '`/books`' handler, however, you should only get one result.

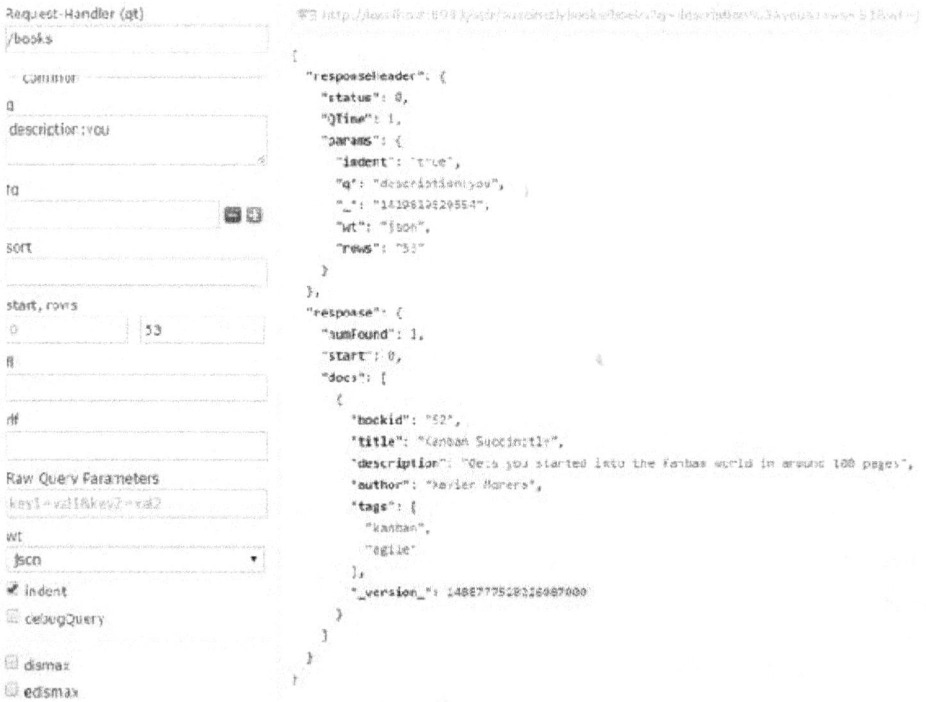

Request-Handler (qt)

/books

common

q

description:you

fq

sort

start, rows
0   53

fl

df

Raw Query Parameters
key1=val1&key2=val2

wt
json   ▼

☑ indent
☐ debugQuery

☐ dismax
☐ edismax

#3 http://localhost:8983/solr/suconnzlybooks/books/?q=description%3Ayou&rows=5&wt=j

[
  "responseheader": {
    "status": 0,
    "QTime": 1,
    "params": {
      "indent": "true",
      "q": "description:you",
      "_": "1419612920554",
      "wt": "json",
      "rows": "53"
    }
  },
  "response": {
    "numFound": 1,
    "start": 0,
    "docs": [
      {
        "bookid": "52",
        "title": "Kanban Succinctly",
        "description": "Gets you started into the Kanban world in around 100 pages",
        "author": "Xavier Morera",
        "tags": [
          "kanban",
          "agile"
        ],
        "_version_": 1486777512326987000
      }
    ]
  }
]

Figure 115: Query results when the '/books' handler is used

Response Fields

Another aspect that you might want to control is which fields are returned in your response for your particular request handler. This is particularly useful when you have a large number of fields. In one of my recent projects, we had about 200 fields per document, of which only about nine are required to be returned on each query for displaying results. So why return them all?

Selecting which fields should be returned is very easy. Basically, within defaults, just add one fl entry and enumerate which fields you want returned.

```
<requestHandler name="/books" class="solr.SearchHandler">
    <lst name="defaults">
        <str name="echoParams">explicit</str>
        <int name="rows">5</int>
        <str name="df">text</str>
        <str name="fl">bookid title description score</str>
    </lst>
    <lst name="appends">
      <str name="fq">author:"Xavier Morera"</str>
    </lst>
</requestHandler>
```

Figure 116: Response fields

Now let's test. First, run a query so you have a baseline. Next, reload the core. Finally, in a separate window, run the same query again. The difference should be clearly visible.

First:

```
{
    "bookid": "52",
    "title": "Kanban Succinctly",
    "description": "Gets you started into the Kanban world in around 100 pages",
    "author": "Xavier Morera",
    "tags": [
      "kanban",
      "agile"
    ],
    "_version_": 1488777528226087000
},
```

Figure 117: First query, no score

After reloading:

```
"docs": [
  {
    "bookid": "52",
    "title": "Kanban Succinctly",
    "description": "Gets you started into the Kanban world in around 100 pages"
    "score": 1
  },
```

Figure 118: Query with score

Facets

Our final small modification will be to return facets. If you recall from previous chapters, Faceting is the arrangement of search results into categories based on indexed terms along with counts that indicate the occurrence of each term. It makes it easier for users to drill down into complex result sets and categorize the information better.

`Facet.query` is an arbitrary query used to generate a facet count. The `facet.field` is used to specify to Solr which field to be treated as a facet. The prefix indicates that only terms that begin with this prefix can be used as a facet.

Let's modify our `/books` request handler within Solrconfig.xml to return facets, and in the process, we will also remove the filter query for author so that we get the entire result set. The steps are simple:

1. Comment out the `appends` section.
2. Add an `invariants` with `facet=true` to enable faceting, and then specify two different facets, `authors` and `tags`. The following XML code should be added to

your config:

```
<lst name="invariants">
<str name="facet">true</str>
        <str name="facet.field">author</str>
    <str name="facet.field">tags</str>
</lst>
```

Your request handler should look like this:

```
<requestHandler name="/books" class="solr.SearchHandler">
    <lst name="defaults">
        <str name="echoParams">explicit</str>
        <int name="rows">5</int>
        <str name="df">text</str>
        <str name="fl">bookid title description score</str>
    </lst>
    <!--
        <lst name="appends">
        <str name="fq">author:"Xavier Morera"</str>
        </lst>
    -->
    <lst name="invariants">
    <str name="facet">true</str>
    <str name="facet.field">author</str>
    <str name="facet.field">tags</str>
    </lst>
</requestHandler>
```

Figure 119: Request handler with facets

Reload the core and run a query for all records with all default values, and scroll down within the response. Here is what you should be looking at:

- The `facet_counts` section includes the resulting facets. In our case, we requested two facet fields, `author` and

tags

. As you can see, they are ordered from highest number of occurrences to lowest. Way to go Ryan with 6. My friend Peter has three books at the time of writing, but my sources tell me he will be tied with Ryan pretty soon!

```
"facet_counts": {
  "facet_queries": {},
  "facet_fields": {
    "author": [
      "Ryan Hodson",
      6,
      "Chris Rose",
      3,
      "Peter Shaw",
      3,
      "Xavier Morera",
      3,
```

Figure 120: Author facet

- Further down, we can see the tags, which by the way, I made up for this exercise. They could be refined further for more realistic results.

```
"tags": [
  "aspnet",
  2,
  "data-structures",
  2,
  "database",
  2,
  "direct3d",
  2,
  "ios",
  2,
  "jquery",
  2,
```

Figure 121: Tags facet

- Finally, we did not include any facet queries, facet dates, facet ranges, or facet intervals.

```
"facet_dates": {},
"facet_ranges": {},
"facet_intervals": {}
}
```

Figure 122: Facets we did not include

You can specify also on multi-valued fields, like tags, and you can also use `facet.mincount` to avoid showing all values below a certain number of hits.

Grouping is also possible with facets. In this case we do not have the number of pages per *Succinctly* series e-book, but if we did, we could dynamically create a range by using the following facets:

- `facet.range=rangepageslong`: Our range.
- `f.pageslong.facet.range.start=0`: The beginning of the range.
- `f.pageslong.facet.range.end=200`: Where I specify the top value of 200.
- `f.pageslong.facet.range=20`: The gap size.

Solr will generate facets with grouped values on the fly!

Your turn: why not give it a shot on your own? Add a column on page size, add the field, reload the core index, and try this exercise!

As mentioned in previous chapters, the admin UI only includes a very small subset of fields. If you want to use the full power of faceting, you need to use the raw query parameters.

Faceting and other operations that need full use of all the fields are generally run from a third-party application, especially ones created to allow administration of the service. Remember though: facets are extremely powerful and useful, and you should attempt to learn all the possible parameters and fields you can, even if just to allow the use of facets.

Solrconfig.Xml Common mistakes and pitfalls

With great power comes great responsibility, and unfortunately, with Solr's config file, you can also do a lot of harm. I've listed some tips for avoiding the common mistakes and pitfalls newcomers make when configuring Solr. Avoiding them will make your search life easier.

- Focus on minimalism. For example, in a schema.xml when you included things that you don't need, the same applies here: only include those things that you need or are planning to use in the near future. Remember: YAGNI (you aren't gonna need it).
- Don't forget caching. Caching is a great tool to increase performance—especially under heavy loads—but it's not always appropriate.
- Avoid overwarming. When Solr starts, you may define some common warming queries. Don't define too many—the more you define, the longer startup takes.
- Don't define too many handlers. You can define too many handlers for each specific scenario, which may over-complicate your deployment, and will make maintenance an absolute nightmare.
- Remember to review the default configuration. The out-of-the-box configuration is not always exactly the best thing for production, so remember to review it before deployment.

- Make sure you upgrade. Solr moves at an incredible pace, so try to keep it up to date, or you might be missing out on some important or interesting features.

Summary

In this section we learned how Solrconfig.xml is the file used to configure Solr's core. We learned how to create a request handler, and then to configure it using appends. Some of the possible configurations involved specifying facets, returned rows, and response fields.

We also learned that every time a change is made in Solrconfig.xml, the core needs to be reloaded from the Admin UI.

Now it's time to learn about searching and relevancy with Solr.

Chapter 8 Searching and Relevance

Do People Love Searching?

When it comes to searching in Solr (and in general), people love searching for things, right? At least, that's the impression we're always given; unfortunately, it's really very far from the truth. The truth is this: People love finding what they're looking for.

As a developer of a search application, it's our job to return the results most relevant to a user's query, and let them fine-tune things from there. While you'll definitely get brownie points if you magically present the user with the results they want the first time, 99 percent of the time, getting very close is good enough.

Relevance

Relevance is the degree to which a query result satisfies the user who is searching for information. It means returning what the user wants or needs. There are basically two important concepts we need to consider when talking about relevance: precision and recall.

Precision

Precision is the percentage of documents in the result set that are relevant to the initial query. That is, how many of the documents contained the results the user was actually looking for. To be clear, we're not talking about exact matches here either; if you're looking for "red cars," matches containing "cars" may still be valid, but matches containing "red paint" would not.

Recall

Recall is the percentage of relevant results returned out of all the relevant results in the system. That is, whether the user got all the documents that in reality matched his or her query. Initially, it is a little bit difficult to understand with a definition, but it becomes a lot simpler with an example:

- You have an index with 10 documents.
- You have a specific query that would match four documents.
- When you run this query, you only get two documents. This means that your recall is not that good, as it is only returning half of the documents that it should.

In real life the scenarios are much more complex; search engines have from thousands to millions of documents, so returning the relevant documents can be difficult.

Obtaining perfect recall is trivial. You simply return every document in the collection for every query, right? But this is a problem if you return every document in the collection—it might not be very useful for the user.

And here is where relevancy comes in. Relevancy is the number of the documents returned by the search engine that are really relevant to your query. To use a real life example, imagine you run a query in Google, and the first page does not return any useful results. None of the results are "relevant" to your query.

There are four scenarios that you need to consider:

- **True Negatives:** These results should never appear in a result set, as they have nothing at all to do with satisfaction of the presented query. A true negative is as bad as it gets for search results; returning them means your search application is not doing its job correctly at all.

- **False positives:** A false positive is when a query matches something in the database, but that match does not relate to the context of the search. Taking our precision example from the previous section, "red paint" would be a false positive—the match occurred due to the use of the term "red," but the context of "paint" does not relate to a context describing cars.

- **False Negatives:** As the name suggests, it's the complete opposite of a false positive. A false negative occurs when a document result matches, but is not returned by the search application. In our previous example, "red car paint" might get rejected on the grounds that its context applies only to paint, and not to a car that's painted red, which is incorrect if our search criteria involves "red cars." When designing your search application, you never want to produce results like this.

- **True positives:** This is the end game—what you're aiming for every time. These are true, context-relevant search results that either satisfy the query, or make it easy to see how the query can be re-organized in order to be better.

Accuracy

This leads to accuracy, which is a tradeoff. In some cases, if you get high precision, you might get very little recall. That is, you might get documents that are extremely relevant to your query, but you might get very few of them. This ultimately results in missing documents that potentially include relevant, but less precise, information for the end user.

At the other end of the spectrum, we have large recall, but with much lower precision. The trick to getting accuracy right is getting the correct balance between these two ends.

Not All Results Are Created Equal

Finally, it is very important to understand that not all results are created equal. When you are configuring your search engine, you need to consider your user's needs.

Context

You need to take into account the categories for each one of the contexts. For example, say you are doing a search for a development company, and you have IT pros and developers. The IT pros might like to get results that are more related to servers and network technologies, while developers might want to look into web development—yet they might be using the same keywords.

Second Page?

It is also important to consider the relevance of the documents. Users rarely go beyond the second page of results, meaning the most relevant results need to be on the first page, with the second page containing the not-so relevant results.

Document Age

In some cases, document age is incredibly important. For example, if you were searching for current news in a newspaper, you only want the most up-to-date results.

Security

A lot of search engineers never give this a second thought, but security is hugely important. I worked on a project for Microsoft a number of years ago where, as part of a security initiative, we had to perform an analysis of approximately 300,000 SharePoint sites. The goal here was to find and prevent unintentional access to confidential company information that the search engine may have returned by mistake. Document security must always be a number one priority.

Speed

Finally, we get to the issue of speed, and the bottom line is this: people expect search results pretty much instantly. A few milliseconds, or maybe even one second, is tolerable for most people. Beyond that, you're going to see complaints—lots of them.

I've seen exceptions where queries could take minutes, but this specific process used to take hours to find the relevant information. This is generally a specialist scenario, where minutes are a massive savings of time, in the bigger scheme of things.

Queries, Data, and Metadata

There are billions of search users worldwide, thanks mainly to Google. However, when you search using Google, you are limited to a small subset of keywords, which includes site, link, related, OR, info, cache, +, -, and other similar operators. If you think about it objectively, this is fine; Google crawls the web, which is kind of a "wild west" humongous set of mainly unstructured data, and not a nice, neatly ordered collection that we might be searching if it was our own data.

Data and Metadata Searching

Within Solr we have more control over our data and the metadata that we have in our index. This allows us to be very accurate and define queries that answer very specific questions. Using our *Succinctly* series data set as an example, we can look for all books by Peter Shaw that talk about Bootstrap.

You would achieve this with the following query:

```
http://localhost:8983/solr/succinctlybooks/books?
q=author%3A%22Peter+Shaw%22+AND+description%3Abootstrap&wt=json&indent=true
```

As you can see in the following figure, we get a very precise and exact match to our query, with only one result.

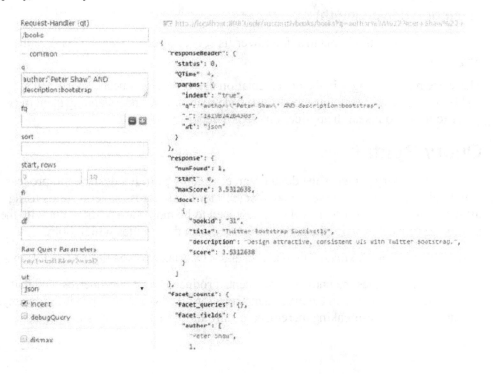

Going Deeper into Solr Search Relevancy

To really understand search and be skilled in tuning search relevancy, it is important to understand the Lucene scoring algorithm, known as the `tf.idf` model. `tf.idf` is an acronym that stands for term frequency, inverse document frequency. The terms are described in the following paragraphs.

tf (Term Frequency)

Term frequency is the frequency in which a term appears in the document or fields. The higher the term frequency, the higher the document score.

idf (Inverse Document Frequency)

The less term appears in other documents in the index, the higher its contribution to the score.

There are two other terms that are not mentioned as part of the name of the scoring algorithm `tf idf`, but are equally important. The terms are as follows:

coord (Coordination Factor)

The more query terms found in the document, the higher the score.

Fieldnorm (Field Length)

The more words a field contains, the lower its score. It penalizes documents with longer field values.

There are multiple pages in the documentation that talk about Lucene scoring. It's highly recommended that you spend some time reading and understanding them in order to make your search applications return better results.

Query Syntax

The DisMax query parser is the default parser used by Solr. It's designed to process simple phrases entered by users, and to search for terms across several fields using different weights or boosts. DisMax is designed to be more Google-like, but with the advantage of working with the highly structured data that resides within Solr.

DisMax stands for Maximum Disjunction, and a DisMax query is defined as follows:

A query that generates the union of documents produced by its sub-queries, and that scores each document with the maximum score for that document as produced by any sub-query, plus a tie-breaking increment for any additional matching sub-queries.

That is a bit of a mouthful—just know that the DisMax query parser was designed to be easy to use and to accept input with less chance of an error.

Let's review some of the possibilities regarding search.

Search for a Word in a Field

Up until now, we've been mostly looking for *:* which meant all searchable fields, all values. You can specify what word or phrases you want to look for, and in which field.

For example, say I want to look for all books that have "database" as part of the description. I would run a query from the Admin UI for **description:database** using the /books request handler as follows:

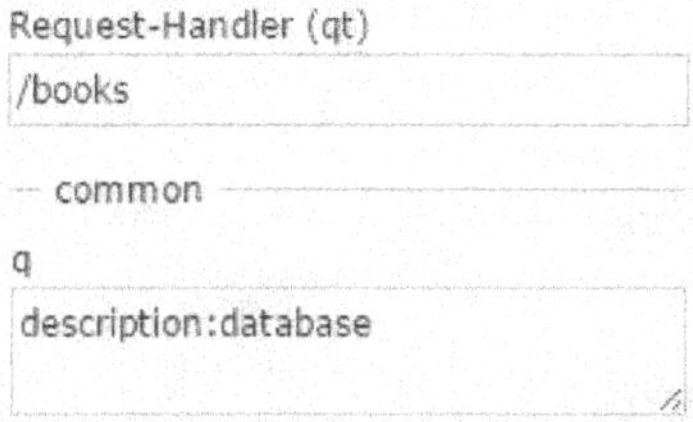

Request-Handler (qt)

/books

— common —

q

description:database

Figure 124: Our example query as it might be viewed using the Admin UI in Solr

The query should give you four results, which you can retrieve to a page of their own using the following URL:

```
http://localhost:8983/solr/succinctlybooks/books?
q=description%3Adatabase&wt=json&indent=true
```

There is something you might notice, however: take a close look at the results returned by the URL, specifically at the score that's returned for each.

The scores returned range from 1.05 to 0.63, which is fine for a general search using wildcards over several fields, but in our case, we're searching for a specific word, in a specific field that we know occurs exactly once in each result. Shouldn't the score in this case be equal for each result?

```
"response": {
  "numFound": 6,
  "start": 0,
  "maxScore": 1.0502609,
  "docs": [
    {
      "bookid": "38",
      "title": "MongoDB Succinctly",
      "description": "Learn to        cDB, the popular open-source database system.",
      "score": 1.0502609
    },
    {
      "bookid": "21",
      "title": "Postgres Succinctly",
      "description": "Learn how         the long-standing open-source Postgres database management system.",
      "score": 0.8402135
    },
    {
      "bookid": "20",
      "title": "Windows Azure SQL Reporting Succinctly",
      "description": "Learn ho        set up a Windows Azure SQL Database server, develop reports, and manage it
      "score": 0.7351868
    },
    {
      "bookid": "32",
      "title": "Node.js Succinctly",
      "description": "Use node        create faster network and server-side applications on any scale, improve
      "score": 0.6301603
    }
  ]
},
```

Figure 125: Different scores for description

Let's test this on a different field and see what happens. This time, we'll search the authors' names for occurrences of my name, using `author:"Xavier Morera"`. Enter the following URL into your browser, making sure to adjust where needed for domain name and port number:

```
http://localhost:8983/solr/succinctlybooks/books?
q=author%3A%22Xavier+Morera%22&wt=json&indent=true
```

This time, we can see that the score for each result is now the same.

Figure 126: Same score for author field

In order to show you what's happening here, we need to repeat the "database" query, but this time, we'll use the debugQuery option to help us. If you're running from the Admin UI, make sure you check the box by **debugQuery** before clicking Execute.

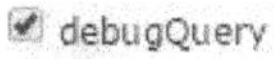

☑ debugQuery

Figure 127: debugQuery Checked

If you're entering the URL directly, make sure you add `debugQuery=true` to the end of the URL before submitting it to your browser:

```
http://localhost:8983/solr/succinctlybooks/books?
q=description%3Adatabase&wt=json&indent=true&debugQuery=true
```

If you scroll down through the results to the debug section, you should see the answer in the **"explain"** section; the **"fieldnorm"** process in Solr is the element that makes all the difference.

```
  "explain":{
    "38":"\n1.0502669 - (MATCH) weight(description:database in 37) [DefaultSimilarity], result of:\n
1.0502669 - fieldWeight in 37, product of:\n    1.0 - tf(freq=1.0) with freq of:\n    1.0 -
termFreq=1.0\n    3.360854 - idf(docFreq=4, maxDocs=53)\n    0.3125 - fieldNorm(doc=37)n",
    "22":"\n0.8402135 - (MATCH) weight(description:database in 21) [DefaultSimilarity], result of:\n
0.8402135 - fieldWeight in 21, product of:\n    1.0 - tf(freq=1.0) with freq of:\n    1.0 -
termFreq=1.0\n    3.360854 - idf(docFreq=4, maxDocs=53)\n    0.25 - fieldNorm(doc=21)n",
    "20":"\n0.7351060 - (MATCH) weight(description:database in 19) [DefaultSimilarity], result of:\n
0.7351868 - fieldWeight in 19, product of:\n    1.0 - tf(freq=1.0) with freq of:\n    1.0 -
termFreq=1.0\n    3.360854 - idf(docFreq=4, maxDocs=53)\n    0.21875 - fieldNorm(doc=19)n",
    "32":"\n0.6301601 - (MATCH) weight(description:database in 31) [DefaultSimilarity], result of:\n
0.6301601 - fieldWeight in 31, product of:\n    1.0 - tf(freq=1.0) with freq of:\n    1.0 -
termFreq=1.0\n    3.360854 - idf(docFreq=4, maxDocs=53)\n    0.1875 - fieldNorm(doc=31)n"},
    "QParser":"LuceneQParser",
```

Figure 128: Fieldnorm makes a difference

Part of the analysis includes `fieldnorm`, which penalizes longer fields. If you look at the following figure, you can see I've drawn a red line across the ends of the descriptions, and you can see that the results at the top (With the more specific score) have shorter descriptions.

Figure 129: Description gets longer as ranking increases

This is just one specific case, where the keyword appeared only once in four documents, and the only difference was the field length. Real-world queries are usually much more complex.

Let's try searching for my name only in authors. This should be something like *"q=Xavier"*; we'll use the following URL and see what happens:

http://localhost:8983/solr/succinctlybooks/select?
q=author%3AXavier&wt=json&indent=true&debugQuery=true

Oddly enough, our query comes back with no results.

```
{
    "responseHeader": {
        "status": 0,
        "QTime": 1,
        "params": {
            "debugQuery": "true",
            "indent": "true",
            "q": "author:Xavier",
            "_": "1419874228687",
            "wt": "json"
        }
    },
    "response": {
        "numFound": 0,
        "start": 0,
        "docs": []
    },
}
```

Figure 130: No results for query Xavier

Initially this might seem like an odd response—after all, we know for sure that my name appears in the `author` field more than once, so how could our query not find anything?

Re-open the Schema.xml file and refresh your memory on the definitions we previously created. You'll see `author` is a `string`, but the description type is `text_general`.

```
<field name="bookid" type="string" indexed="true" stored="true" required="true" multiValued="false" />
<field name="title" type="text_general" indexed="true" stored="true"/>
<field name="description" type="text_general" indexed="true" stored="true"/>
<field name="author" type="string" indexed="true" stored="true"/>
<field name="tags" type="string" indexed="true" stored="true" multiValued="true"/>
```

Figure 131: Author is string and description is text_general

It's the field type that makes the difference; `string` is a simple type, storing just a simple text string. To find it, you need to run a query for an exact match. This is great for faceting, but not so good for general searching.

However, `text_general` is a complex type, as it has `analyzers`, `tokenizers`, and `filters`. Additionally, within `analyzers`, it has both `query` and `index` time. Its main use is for general purpose text searching.

Once you understand the different field types, things get much easier.

Search for a Phrase in a Field

As we did previously with the author field, we can search for phrases. Let's try to use our `description:database` query and refine it further by querying for `description:"database system"`.

We can easily do this using the following query:

```
http://localhost:8983/solr/succinctlybooks/books?
q=description%3A%22database+system%22&wt=json&indent=true&debugQuery=true
```

We only got one exact match. Fantastic, our search works and gives us exact results, right? Not quite, as we don't really want to be absolutely specific when doing general searches.

```
{
  "bookid": "38",
  "title": "MongoDB Succinctly",
  "description": "Learn to use MongoDB, the popular open-source database system.",
  "score": 2.1005337
}
```

Figure 132: Exact match search

Proximity

What if we wanted to find not an exact match, but a match in close proximity? For example, *MongoDB Succinctly* had `"database system"`, but that left out *Postgres Succinctly*, which had `"database management system"`, which is a very close match that could be useful for our users.

To address this, we have something called proximity matching, otherwise known as the process of finding words that are within a specific distance of our match word.

Change the query we just issued (the one that only returned one result) so that our `q` parameter now reads `'q = description:"database system"~4'`. If you are entering this via a URL in your browser, the new query should look as follows:

```
http://localhost:8983/solr/succinctlybooks/books?
q=description%3A%22database+system%22~4&wt=json&indent=true&debugQuery=true
```

As you can see in the following figure, we now have two results, and more importantly, our score gives us an idea of the order of importance or relevance.

```
{
  "bookid": "38",
  "title": "MongoDB Succinctly",
  "description": "Learn to use MongoDB, the popular open-source database system.",
  "score": 2.1005337
},
{
  "bookid": "22",
  "title": "Postgres Succinctly",
  "description": "Learn how to use the long-standing open-source Postgres database management system.",
  "score": 1.1882412
}
```

Figure 133: Proximity search

Operators and Fields

It's possible to use operators for querying. For example, if I want to search for all books that have a description of databases AND use Azure as a technology, I would form my query term as `'description:database AND description:Azure'`. Converting this to a URL, we end up with the following:

```
http://localhost:8983/solr/succinctlybooks/books?
q=description%3Adatabase+AND+description%3AAzure&wt=json&indent=true&debugQ
```

As you might expect, you can also do an OR search. For example, the following query term `'description:database OR description:Azure'`, turned into the following URL:

```
http://localhost:8983/solr/succinctlybooks/books?
q=description%3Adatabase+OR+description%3AAzure&wt=json&indent=true&debugQu
```

This yields four results. You can also match between fields, for example, searching for all books with tags `'aspnet'` or with `'Net'` in the title. The query term would be `'tags:aspnet OR title:net'`, and the following URL demonstrates this:

```
http://localhost:8983/solr/succinctlybooks/select?
q=tags%3Aaspnet+OR+title%3Anet&wt=json&indent=true
```

You can nest operators as much as you need to, but you **must** remember capitalization. It's different to use AND vs and; this is an important point. If you get the capitalization wrong, your search won't work as expected.

Not (Negative Queries)

It's also possible to perform a negative search, that is, a search where you specifically request NOT to include results for a given term. For example, you could search for *tags:aspnet*, and you will get two results: *ASP.NET MVC 4 Mobile Websites* and *ASP.NET Web API*. If we don't want any results that relate to mobile, we can use the following query term (notice the - symbol):

```
tags:aspnet AND -title:Mobile
```

In URL format, it will look like this:

```
http://localhost:8983/solr/succinctlybooks/books?q=tags%3Aaspnet+AND+-
title%3AMobile&wt=json&indent=true
```

Try altering the URL to include only `'tags:aspnet'` then include the `'AND -title:Mobile'`. Note that the first form gives two results, and the second only gives one result, just as we might expect.

```
▼<response>
  ▼<lst name="responseHeader">
      <int name="status">0</int>
      <int name="QTime">4</int>
    ▼<lst name="params">
        <str name="indent">true</str>
        <str name="q">tags:aspnet AND -title:Mobile</str>
        <str name="wt">xml</str>
      </lst>
  </lst>
  ▼<result name="response" numFound="1" start="0" maxScore="3.8716795">
    ▼<doc>
        <str name="bookid">24</str>
        <str name="title">ASP.NET Web API Succinctly</str>
      ▼<str name="description">
          Microsoft's ASP.NET Web API simplifies data delivery through HTTP.
        </str>
        <float name="score">3.8716795</float>
      </doc>
  </result>
```

Figure 134: Negative query result showing only one match

Wildcard Matching

As you've already seen in many places in this book (*:*), we've used wildcards quite a lot so far. There's more to wildcards than you might realize, however. Solr supports using wildcards at the end and in the middle of a word. A **?** means a variation of a single character, while * means many characters.

In case you're wondering, a '*' at the beginning of a phrase (called a leading wildcard or suffix query) was originally NOT supported in Solr. This has recently been changed, but please know that it's an incredibly inefficient search method, and not recommended for production use.

Let's try some example wildcard searches. Create some searches (either in the Admin UI or with a browser URL) using the following query terms:

- author:"Xavier*"
- author:Xavier*
- author:X*a
- author:*Morera

Try creating some URLs of your own to satisfy these queries, or simply just use the Admin UI. Once you understand how the position affects the operator, scroll down to see if your results match those in the following table.

Query	Result	Notes

author:"Xavier*"	`{`
	  `"responseHeader": {`
	    `"status": 0,`
	    `"QTime": 0,`
	    `"params": {`
	      `"indent": "true",`
	      `"q": "author:\"Xavier*\" ",`
	      `"_": "1420571941955",`
	      `"wt": "json"`
	    `}`
	  `},`
	  `"response": {`
	    `"numFound": 0,`
		This query has zero results as you are doing a phrase search.

author:Xavier*	`{`
	  `"responseHeader": {`
	    `"status": 0,`
	    `"QTime": 5,`
	    `"params": {`
	      `"indent": "true",`
	      `"q": "author:Xavier* ",`
	      `"_": "1420571758690",`
	      `"wt": "json"`
	    `}`
	  `},`
	  `"response": {`
	    `"numFound": 3,`
		Remove the quotes and we get the expected results.

author:X*a	`{`
	  `"responseHeader": {`
	    `"status": 0,`
	    `"QTime": 379,`
	    `"params": {`
	      `"indent": "true",`
	      `"q": "author:X*a",`
	      `"_": "1420571984291",`
	      `"wt": "json"`
	    `}`
	  `},`
	  `"response": {`
	    `"numFound": 3,`
		Works fine, as expected. Solr returns any author that starts with x and ends with a.

author:*Morera	{
	    "responseHeader": {
	        "status": 0,
	        "QTime": 10,
	        "params": {
	            "indent": "true",
	            "q": "author:*Morera",
	            "_": "1420572021654",
	            "wt": "json"
	        }
	    },
	    "response": {
	        "numFound": 3,
		This gives us the results we expected, but remember placing the '*' in front of the term is inefficient.

Due to the small sizes of our index and search data in these examples, we don't see a great deal of difference in the query times. However, if we had a larger data set and index, you would easily be able to see which methods are the most efficient.

Range Searches

Range queries allow matching of documents with values within a specified range of values. In our example, we haven't included any dates (or for that matter, any range-based data); if we had done so, in a field called createddate for example, we could have performed a query that looked something like:

```
createddate:[20120101 TO 20130101]
```

This would have allowed us to search the field createddate for results that were contained in the lower and upper bounds enclosed by the square brackets. Here are a few more range examples.

- field:[* TO 100] retrieves all field values less than or equal to 100
- field:[100 TO *] retrieves all field values greater than or equal to 100
- field:[* TO *] matches all documents with the field

Boosts

Query time boosts allow us to define the importance of each field. For example, if you run a query for a specific term, and you are more interested in that term appearing in the title than in the description of the document, you might form a query term that looks like this:

```
title:javascript^1.5 description:javascript
```

In this case, you are applying a boost of "1.5" to whenever your term appears in the title, while still remaining interested if it is also present in the description.

I recommend that you use explain so that you can see how your boosting affects scoring. In our initial tour of the Admin UI in the query section, we mentioned that there is a checkbox called debug query that is used to display debug information. Enable it, and the response will come with a text that explains why a particular document is a match, or relevant, to your query. In this particular case, you can see boost being used to affect the score of your document.

```
▼<str name="5">
    2.996006 = (MATCH) sum of: 2.2887545 = (MATCH) weight(title:javascript^1.5 in 4) [DefaultSimilarity],
    0.85618025 = queryWeight, product of: 1.5 = boost 4.277145 = idf(docFreq=1, maxDocs=53) 0.13345043 = c
    freq of: 1.0 = termFreq=1.0 4.277145 = idf(docFreq=1, maxDocs=53) 0.625 = fieldNorm(doc=4) 0.7072514 =
    0.7072514 = score(doc=4,freq=2.0 = termFreq=2.0 ), product of: 0.5166773 = queryWeight, product of: 0.
    fieldWeight in 4, product of: 1.4142135 = tf(freq=2.0), with freq of: 2.0 = termFreq=2.0 3.8716795 = i
</str>
```

Figure 135: Boosting affects scoring

Boosting does not need to be performed on every query; likewise, every query is not performed only on the default field(df). You can specify the query fields (qf) in your Solrconfig.Xml, so that on every query, the desired boosts are applied automatically.

The following figure shows an example of a handler for the built-in sample collection (the collection we used before we defined our Succinctly books collection). As you can see, the handler has pre-specified which boosts should be applied when searching, and to which fields it should be applied automatically.

```
<str name="qf">
text^0.5 features^1.0 name^1.2 sku^1.5 id^10.0 manu^1.1 cat^1.4
title^10.0 description^5.0 keywords^5.0 author^2.0 resourcename^1.0
</str>
```

Figure 136: Boost specified in handler

This is the essence of how you tweak your Solr application. You make small changes over time and analyze the results, log the searches your users are performing, then try the tweaks yourself against those searches. This process of trial and error can be tedious, but in the search industry in particular, it's often the best way to fine-tune things to provide the expected results.

It is important to take into consideration that df is only used when qf is not specified.

Keyword Search and CopyFields

Up until now, we've been doing mostly queries within fields, for example, author:Xavier Morera.

Imagine, however, that we wanted to search just for a keyword, such as "Succinctly." This one should match all of the books in our collection, right? After all, every book in the series has this word in its title.

Not quite. Run a query from the Admin UI for the term 'Succinctly' and observe the results.

Request-Handler (qt)

/books

—— common ——

q

succinctly

fq

■ ⊡

sort

start, rows

0   10

fl

df

🔲 http://localhost:8983/solr/succinct/books/books?q=succinctly

{
    "responseHeader": {
        "status": 0,
        "QTime": 4,
        "params": {
            "debugQuery": "true",
            "indent": "true",
            "q": "succinctly",
            "_": "1420573366972",
            "wt": "json"
        }
    },
    "response": {
        "numFound": 0,
        "start": 0,
        "maxScore": 0,
        "docs": []
    },

Figure 137: No results for query "Succinctly"

Why are no results returned? It's very simple—let's take a look at our Solrconfig.xml file right now to find an answer. Please find the /books request handler. As we can see in the following figure, we have a df of text. df stands for default field; therefore, we are telling Solr that our default search field is called *text*.

```
<requestHandler name="/books" class="solr.SearchHandler">
    <lst name="defaults">
        <str name="echoParams">explicit</str>
        <int name="rows">5</int>
        <str name="df">text</str>
        <str name="fl">bookid title description score</str>
    </lst>
```

Figure 138: Text is our default field

But if you look within Schema.xml for the copy field declaration for text, you will notice that it is commented out. Therefore, it is empty now, as no information is copied over to text during indexing.

```
<!-- catchall field, containing all other searchable text fields (implemented
    via copyField further on in this schema -->
<field name="text" type="text_general" indexed="true" stored="false" multiValued="true"/>
```

Figure 139: All copy fields commented out

Let's give it a try and modify the df so that it points to the description, which can be done in Solrconfig.xml. As you can see in the following figure, df has a value of description instead of text. Don't forget to reload the core or restart Solr.

```
<requestHandler name="/books" class="solr.SearchHandler">
    <lst name="defaults">
        <str name="echoParams">explicit</str>
        <int name="rows">5</int>
        <str name="df">description</str>
        <str name="fl">bookid title description score</str>
    </lst>
```

Figure 140: Change default field to description

If we now re-run our previous query following the changes we made to our
configuration, we should now see that we get much better results.

Figure 141: Run query again

If you wish to use the direct URL, just enter the following into your browser:

```
http://localhost:8983/solr/succinctlybooks/books?
q=succinctly&wt=json&indent=true&debugQuery=true
```

In this case, we are searching in a single field, so let's revert back to text and create a
copyField for each one we would like to have copied. This is done in the
Schema.xml file.

```
<copyField source="title" dest="text"/>
<copyField source="description" dest="text"/>
<copyField source="author" dest="text"/>
<copyField source="tags" dest="text"/>
```

Figure 142: Copy fields

Reload and query again. You'll notice it did not work—but why?

```
{
  "responseHeader": {
    "status": 0,
    "QTime": 5,
    "params": {
      "debugQuery": "true",
      "indent": "true",
      "q": "succinctly",
      "_": "1420577047118",
      "wt": "json"
    }
  },
  "response": {
    "numFound": 0,
    "start": 0,
    "maxScore": 0,
    "docs": []
  },
```

Figure 143: Query did not work

This is the query:

```
http://localhost:8983/solr/succinctlybooks/books?
q=succinctly&wt=json&indent=true&debugQuery=true
```

The **`copyField`** is done when a document is indexed, so it is before the index analyzer. It is the same process as if you provided the same input text in two different fields. In a nutshell, you need reindexing.

Reindex the way that you did using *exercise-1-succinctly-schema-index.bat* from exampledocs, from the command line.

```
C:\solr-succinctly\succinctly\exampledocs>java -Durl=http://localhost:8983/solr/succ
ema.csv"
SimplePostTool version 1.5
Posting files to base url http://localhost:8983/solr/succinctlybooks/update using co
POSTing file exercise-1-succinctly-schema.csv
1 files indexed.
COMMITting Solr index changes to http://localhost:8983/solr/succinctlybooks/update..
Time spent: 0:00:00.244
```

Figure 144: Reindex sample data

Run the query again. How many results should you get?

Request-Handler (qt)

/books

--- common ---

q

succinctly

fq

sort

start, rows

0   10

fl

🖵 http://localhost:8983/solr/succinctlybooks/books?q=succinctly

{
  "responseHeader": {
    "status": 0,
    "QTime": 12,
    "params": {
      "debugQuery": "true",
      "indent": "true",
      "q": "succinctly",
      "_": "1420577568034",
      "wt": "json"
    }
  },
  "response": {
    "numFound": 50,
    "start": 0,
    "maxScore": 0.32125914,
    "docs": [

Figure 145: Query again with 50 results

The answer is 50. Why? We have 53 documents, but the reindexing only considers our initial result set. We manually added the other three.

Synonyms

Synonyms are used in Solr to match words or phrases that have the same meaning. It allows you to match strings of tokens and replace them with other strings of tokens, in order to help increase recall. Synonym mappings can also be used to correct misspellings. Let's try a simple test to illustrate what I mean.

> *Tip: To make sure that we have all of our sample data in our index, please open a command prompt, navigate to solr-succinctly\succinctly\exampledocs, and run the following batch file: exercise-1-succinctly-schema-index-fixseparator.bat. By doing so, you will reload the sample books into your index.*

Run a query for q=lightning on our books collection; you should see no results found.

{
  "responseHeader": {
    "status": 0,
    "QTime": 11,
    "params": {
      "debugQuery": "true",
      "indent": "true",
      "q": "lightning",
      "_": "1420579892487",
      "wt": "json"
    }
  },
  "response": {
    "numFound": 0,
    "start": 0,
    "maxScore": 0,
    "docs": []

Now open Schema.Xml for the succinctlybooks collection, and go to our default field type, `text_general`. You can find it within the `fieldtype name=text_general` node, as you can see in the following figure. Within the `analyzer` node of `type=query`, you can see a `filter` of `class=solr.SynonymFilterFactory`. This indicates that your Solr has synonyms configured for any fields of type `text_general` that are calculated at query time.

Great! That means no re-indexing is needed, although it might potentially affect performance at a certain scale.

```
<fieldType name="text_general" class="solr.TextField" positionIncrementGap="100">
  <analyzer type="index">
    <tokenizer class="solr.StandardTokenizerFactory"/>
    <filter class="solr.StopFilterFactory" ignoreCase="true" words="stopwords.txt" />
    <!-- in this example, we will only use synonyms at query time
    <filter class="solr.SynonymFilterFactory" synonyms="index_synonyms.txt" ignoreCase="true" expand="false"/>
    -->
    <filter class="solr.LowerCaseFilterFactory"/>
  </analyzer>
  <analyzer type="query">
    <tokenizer class="solr.StandardTokenizerFactory"/>
    <filter class="solr.StopFilterFactory" ignoreCase="true" words="stopwords.txt" />
    <filter class="solr.SynonymFilterFactory" synonyms="synonyms.txt" ignoreCase="true" expand="true"/>
    <filter class="solr.LowerCaseFilterFactory"/>
  </analyzer>
</fieldType>
```

Figure 147: Review text_general

If you look closely at the filter for the synonyms, it has an `attribute` `synonyms="synonyms.txt"`. This means that our synonyms dictionary is this text file, which is located in our **conf** directory for the succinctlybooks core.

Name	Date modified	Type	Size
spellings.txt	10/26/2014 5:57 AM	Text Document	1 KB
stopwords.txt	10/26/2014 5:57 AM	Text Document	1 KB
synonyms.txt	1/6/2015 3:31 PM	Text Document	2 KB

Figure 148: Location of synonyms.txt

Open the file and add an entry (like for `lightning`) so that it is used as a synonym for `bootstrap`. We have comma-separated values.

`lightning,bootstrap`

You should have something similar to the following:

```
#-----------------------------------------------------------------
#some test synonym mappings unlikely to appear in real input text
aaafoo => aaabar
bbbfoo => bbbfoo bbbbar
ccccfoo => cccbar cccbaz
fooaaa,baraaa,bazaaa

# Some synonym groups specific to this example
lightning,bootstrap
GB,gib,gigabyte,gigabytes
MB,mib,megabyte,megabytes
Television, Televisions, TV, TVs
#notice we use "gib" instead of "GiB" so any WordDelimiterFilter coming
#after us won't split it into two words.

# Synonym mappings can be used for spelling correction too
pixima => pixma
```

Figure 149: Synonyms.txt file contents

Now try running the query for `lightning` again, using the `/books` request handler in the succinctlybooks core. You should get no results. As with most configuration changes, you'll need to reload the core for things to take effect.

```
{
  "responseHeader": {
    "status": 0,
    "QTime": 9,
    "params": {
      "debugQuery": "true",
      "indent": "true",
      "q": "lightning",
      "_": "1420580314164",
      "wt": "json"
    }
  },
  "response": {
    "numFound": 1,
    "start": 0,
    "maxScore": 1.2080518,
    "docs": [
      {
        "bookid": "31",
        "title": "Twitter Bootstrap Succinctly",
        "description": "Design attractive, consistent UIs with Twitter Bootstrap.",
        "score": 1.2080518
      }
    ]
  },
```

Figure 150: Reload and query for lightning

Now, my friend Peter Shaw's Bootstrap book is there. (Which I personally recommend to every single developer who, like me, is UI challenged! It really makes a difference.)

Stopwords

Stopwords are how Solr deals with removing common words from a query. Common words are defined as standard English common words such as 'a', 'an', 'and', 'are', and 'as', along with many others. Any word that is likely to be commonly found in every sentence could be classed as a stopword.

In some cases, a word does not have any special meaning within a specific index. In our case, all documents have the word "succinctly," so it provides no additional value when used. In a previous project that I worked on, I had to index all patents and applications worldwide; this lead to the word "patent" not having any special meaning.

Let's try a query with `q=succinctly`. You should get the following results:

```
{
  "responseHeader": {
    "status": 0,
    "QTime": 8,
    "params": {
      "debugQuery": "true",
      "indent": "true",
      "q": "succinctly",
      "_": "1420580861241",
      "wt": "json"
    }
  },
  "response": {
    "numFound": 50,
    "start": 0,
    "maxScore": 0.32125914,
    "docs": [
```

Figure 151: Query for succinctly

Please remember that you can construct the URL for this query from the Admin UI, by running a query and clicking on the gray box at the top right.

Figure 152: Where to click to construct query URL

All results are found, as the word occurs in every single document. The way to indicate which words should not be used in a query is via stopwords. This is done via the Solr.stopfilterfactory.

To add a **stopword**, you need to go to the **conf** directory, in the same location where we modified our synonyms.

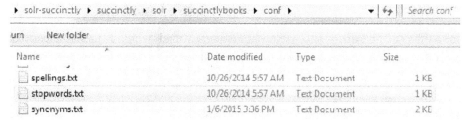

Figure 153: Location of stopwords.txt

Open **stopwords.txt** and add the desired word.

```
 1   # Licensed to the Apache Software Foundation (ASF) under one or more
 2   # contributor license agreements.  See the NOTICE file distributed with
 3   # this work for additional information regarding copyright ownership.
 4   # The ASF licenses this file to You under the Apache License, Version 2.0
 5   # (the "License"); you may not use this file except in compliance with
 6   # the License.  You may obtain a copy of the License at
 7   #
 8   #     http://www.apache.org/licenses/LICENSE-2.0
 9   #
10   # Unless required by applicable law or agreed to in writing, software
11   # distributed under the License is distributed on an "AS IS" BASIS,
12   # WITHOUT WARRANTIES OR CONDITIONS OF ANY KIND, either express or implied.
13   # See the License for the specific language governing permissions and
14   # limitations under the License.
15   succinctly
16
```

Figure 154: Contents of stopwords.txt

If you run the query now, all documents should still be returned, which means that the stopwords are not working. This is expected, because we just made a configuration change, but have not yet reloaded the core as required.

```
{
  "responseHeader": {
    "status": 0,
    "QTime": 4,
    "params": {
      "debugQuery": "true",
      "indent": "true",
      "q": "succinctly",
      "_": "1420581219464",
      "wt": "json"
    }
  },
  "response": {
    "numFound": 0,
    "start": 0,
    "maxScore": 0,
    "docs": []
```

Figure 155: No results yet

Reload the core and query again. No results were found, which is the outcome we expected.

Stopwords can be added both at query and at index time. It's very useful at index time because if these words are removed from your index and they are very common, it helps with the index size. At query time, it is also useful, as no reindexing is required.

Summary

In this section, we have learned some of the basics of searching using Solr. This is an extremely large subject that could spawn hundreds or even thousands of pages, but this kick-start puts you in a nice position to move forward on your own.

In the next section, we will discuss user interfaces with Solr.

Chapter 9 Add a UI

Solr can be used in many different ways. In a lot of cases, you can use it as a small functionality within your application. For example, it can be used to implement a type ahead function as an aid to the end user. In other cases, your application might be more search-centric, for example, a patent analysis application to find prior art.

In any case, and irrespective of your current requirements, it's highly likely that at some point you'll need a custom user interface for Solr. In this chapter I present two well-known alternatives that will make that task much easier.

Solritas: A Fancy Name for Velocity ResponseWriter

Now that you know how to create your own custom handlers, there is one that I'd like to direct your interest to, as it can help you create your own search applications. The `/browse` request handler is already present in your application. Open your Solrconfig.xml and find it; it should look something like the following image.

```
<requestHandler name="/browse" class="solr.SearchHandler">
    <lst name="defaults">
        <str name="echoParams">explicit</str>

        <!-- VelocityResponseWriter settings -->
        <str name="wt">velocity</str>
        <str name="v.template">browse</str>
        <str name="v.layout">layout</str>
        <str name="title">Solritas</str>

        <!-- Query settings -->
        <str name="defType">edismax</str>
        <str name="qf">
    text^0.5 features^1.0 name^1.2 sku^1.5 id^10.0 manu^1.1 cat^1.4
    title^10.0 description^5.0 keywords^5.0 author^2.0 resourcename^1.0
        </str>
        <str name="df">text</str>
        <str name="mm">100%</str>
        <str name="q.alt">*:*</str>
        <str name="rows">10</str>
        <str name="fl">*,score</str>

        <str name="mlt.qf">
    text^0.5 features^1.0 name^1.2 sku^1.5 id^10.0 manu^1.1 cat^1.4
    title^10.0 description^5.0 keywords^5.0 author^2.0 resourcename^1.0
        </str>
        <str name="mlt.fl">text,features,name,sku,id,manu,cat,title,description,
```

Figure 156: Velocity ResponseWriter

The Velocity ResponseWriter, also known as Solritas, is a handler that allows processing of results with the use of the template system called Velocity.

You can read more at http://velocity.apache.org/. It has not been updated recently, but you can use it to learn a lot about querying, geolocation, and much more. Velocity is a very quick and easy way to generate a UI for testing your data. To access it, simply navigate to the following:

```
http://localhost:8983/solr/browse
```

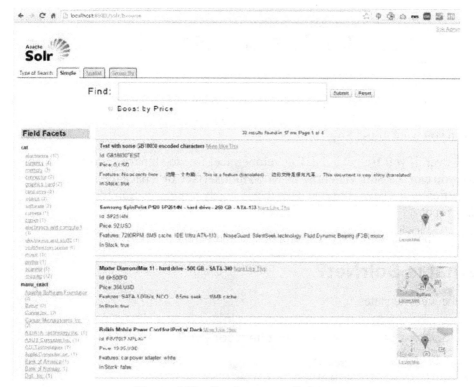

Figure 157: Also known as Solritas

Your turn: Why not try modifying it with the Succinctly collection? I would recommend adding a `publicationdate` field in Schema.Xml. Then, add random dates for all the books in our sample data file, books.csv, index, and test. Branch in GitHub and give it a shot to learn how it works. It includes geolocation and boosting.

SolrNet: An Apache Solr Client for .NET

I have been a .NET developer since the early days of .NET Beta. If you are one too, then this chapter will be of high interest to you, as SolrNet is an excellent choice when you want to use Solr from .NET.

However, if you are not a .NET developer, feel free to skip the rest of this chapter, and you can use Solr via either its RESTful interface or a package created specifically for your language. One that is highly popular is SolrJ for Java developers.

But for those that are .NET developers, lo and behold, we have SolrNet.

What is SolrNet?

As the website states:

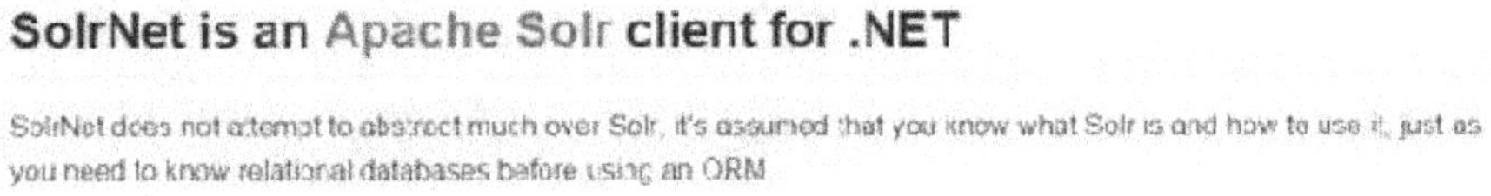

SolrNet is an Apache Solr client for .NET

SolrNet does not attempt to abstract much over Solr, it's assumed that you know what Solr is and how to use it, just as you need to know relational databases before using an ORM

Figure 158: SolrNet is an Apache client for .NET

For a .NET developer, SolrNet helps you work with Solr in a very natural way, by allowing you to represent your schema via the use of Plain Old CLR Objects (POCOs). If you are not familiar with POCOs, they are basically a class that represents exactly what we have in our Schema.XML, type-for-type, with the exact same names.

SolrNet makes Solr feel part of your code in a way that a RESTful interface really can't.

SolrNet's History

SolrNet was created by Mauricio Scheffer, from Argentina, in 2007. I contacted him personally and asked about the history of Solr. He pointed me to the original blog post where he first introduced SolrNet, which can be found here.

He also gave me an overview of how SolrNet was born. He had a requirement to add facets to a site he was working on at the time, but due to other commitments with work, he did not have time to act on it, so he was paid an additional sum of money to complete the work outside normal office hours. As part of the project, he negotiated the release of the code as open source.

He originally posted to code.google.com, but as it has become favorable with many open source projects, it now lives in GitHub.

At the time, Solr was on version 1.2, meaning it was an early release, and one which had very little documentation. He based some of his work on SolrSharp, which by this point had fallen into an in-active state. His main driving force, however, was the desire to add unit tests and improve the overall build of the library.

In any case, thank you Mauricio! Also, special thanks for responding to my messages with the insight and information you did, allowing me to share the story with my readers.

Getting SolrNet

To get SolrNet, simply clone it from GitHub: https://github.com/mausch/SolrNet

If you don't know Git, there are two things you can do. One is to just click **Download** to get a local copy of the code, and the second is to get the *Git Succinctly* e-book. Git is an amazing tool that you should not ignore.

Figure 159: Getting SolrNet

My Git client of choice is SourceTree, but feel free to use whichever makes you more comfortable.

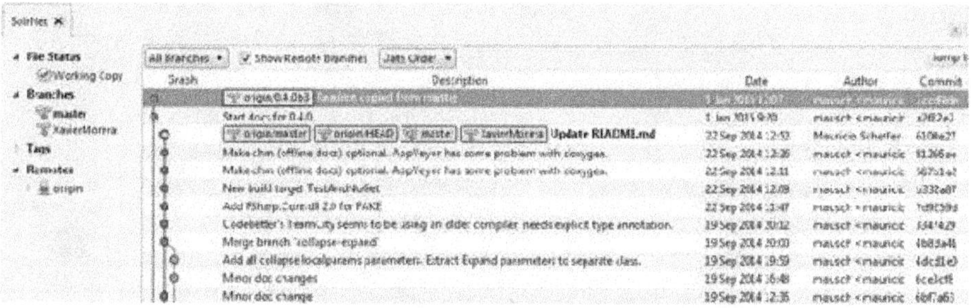

Figure 160: SourceTree as Git client

There's an old URL in code.google.com; it's the original repository that is still alive, but no longer maintained, so ignore it.

SolrNet

Once you have SolrNet, there are several ways to get it up and running. You will need Visual Studio. I have 2012, but it works with other versions as well, including Visual Studio Community.

SolrNet comes with a sample .NET application. You can use this as a base to create your own Solr application, or just as a testing ground for your Solr configuration and development.

It comes in the form of a standard ASP.NET MVC application. If you're not familiar with ASP.NET MVC, you may have a few other concepts to learn to get started; the SampleSolrApp teaches you very well how to use SolrNet.

My usual workflow is to first open the main SolrNet project and build the solution, just to check that everything is present and working ok.

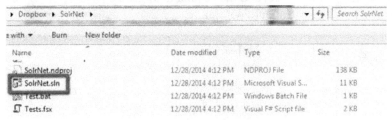

Figure 161: SolrNet solution

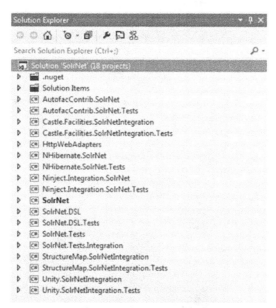

Figure 162: SolrNet projects

If everything goes well, you should get a successful build report.

Figure 163: Rebuild succeeded

Once you're happy that SolrNet is working ok, close that project and open the solution for the sample application. As shown in the following figure, select to rebuild the solution as you did with SolrNet.

Name	Date modified	Type	Size
ReSharper.CodingStyle.xml	12/28/2014 4:12 PM	XML Document	19 KB
runsample.bat	12/28/2014 4:12 PM	Windows Batch File	1 KB
SampleSolrApp.sln	12/28/2014 4:12 PM	Microsoft Visual S...	2 KB
SolrNet.5.1.ReSharper	12/28/2014 4:12 PM	RESHARPER File	5 KB
SolrNet.6.0.ReSharper	12/28/2014 4:12 PM	RESHARPER File	5 KB

Figure 164: Open SampleSolrApp

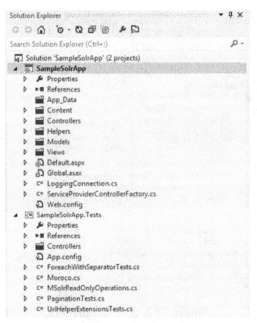

Figure 165: Rebuild solution

At this point, you should expect to get some build errors in the solution.

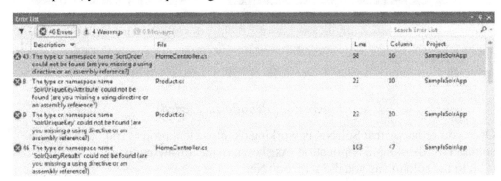

Figure 166: Errors on rebuild

If you look in the project references, you'll see that you need to re-link the newly rebuilt SolrNet assembly.

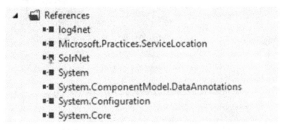

Figure 167: Problem with SolrNet

I know this means there is a warning, so I hide my errors.

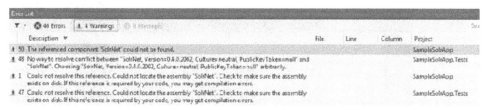

Figure 168: Missing assembly

You can fix this by re-binding the reference to SolrNet.dll, which can be found in
SolrNet\bin\Debug.

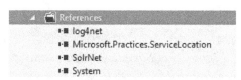

Figure 169: Get assembly and problem solved

If you rebuild again after adding the reference, you'll find you still have a couple
more things to fix.

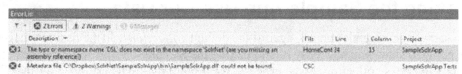

Figure 170: New errors with SolrNet.DSL

Add `solrNet.DSL` from `SolrNet.DSL\bin\Debug` to fix the remaining issues, then
rebuild and run.

Figure 171: Rebuild successful for SampleSolrApp

If everything has worked, you should be greeted with the following web application:

Figure 172: SampleSolrApp running

Go ahead and play around, run queries, and analyze responses. View how facets, paging, and items per page affect queries. Put in a breakpoint or two. Compare it with what you have in the Admin UI.

Making the Sample App Use Our Data

The sample is currently running against the default *collection1*. In the next few pages, I'm going to show you how easy it is to modify the SampleSolrApp so that it uses our succinctlybooks collection. In the process, we'll build our own custom UI for the Syncfusion *Succinctly* series.

I will give you an initial step and a few tips. Let's get started.

1. Make sure you have a running Solr instance populated with our sample succinctly data. If you need to rebuild, you can get a new install from my GitHub page at https://github.com/xaviermorera/solr-succinctly.

2. In the Web.Config of SampleSolrApp that's shipped with SolrNet, find the `solrUrl` key and change it to use the succinctly collection:

```
<add key="solrUrl" value="http://localhost:8983/solr/succinctlybooks" />
```

3. At this point, if you run the SolrNet app, you will get an application error as follows:

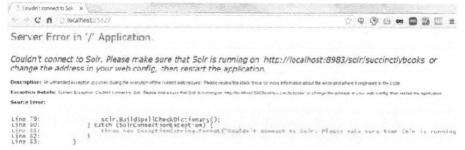

Figure 173: Error connecting to Solr

4. Open Solr's log, and you will see the error. It all makes sense now. You are trying to read from succinctlybooks using collection1 schema. How do I know? Please look at the following figure. Solr did not tell me directly, but it hinted me in the right direction by stating `"document is missing mandatory field bookid"`. I realized I had documents in my index that did not have the unique key, meaning that they are from another collection. It may seem hard at this moment, but once you get experience, you will be able to pick out these errors much easier.

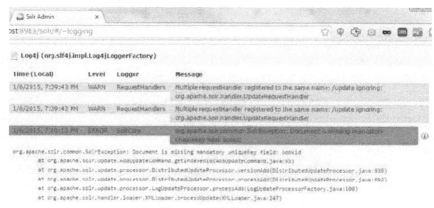

Figure 174: Solr Log

5. Don't believe me completely? Use the best trick in the book while debugging: turn on Break on Exceptions. Quick access is via Ctrl+Alt+E in Visual Studio. Visual Studio does not tell you when an exception is raised and caught. However, if you turn on Break on Exceptions, you will be prompted whenever any exception occurs in the exact line.

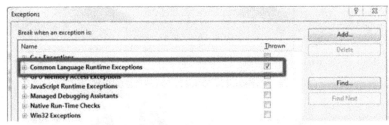

Figure 175: Turn on Break on Exception

Now you can clearly see that the real exception is being masked.

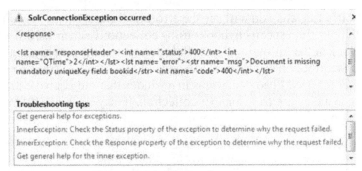

Figure 176: The real exception

If you've gotten to this point, you are on the right path. Here are a few tips on next steps:

- The sample apps uses a function called `AddInitialDocuments` to populate with sample data. We don't need it in the succinctlybooks collection, so comment it out.

- You need to modify your POCO to match your Solr schema.xml. It is currently defined in `Product.cs`, as shown in the following figure.

```
Product.cs ⊖ ✱ ×
⟨⟩ SampleSolrApp.Models.Product
  ⊟namespace SampleSolrApp.Models {
  ⊟    public class Product {
            [SolrUniqueKey("id")]
            public string Id { get; set; }

            [SolrField("sku")]
            public string SKU { get; set; }

            [SolrField("name")]
            public string Name { get; set; }

            [SolrField("manu_exact")]
            public string Manufacturer { get; set; }

            [SolrField("cat")]
            public ICollection<string> Categories { get; set; }

            [SolrField("features")]
            public ICollection<string> Features { get; set; }

            [SolrField("price")]
            public decimal Price { get; set; }

            [SolrField("popularity")]
            public int Popularity { get; set; }

            [SolrField("inStock")]
            public bool InStock { get; set; }

            [SolrField("timestamp")]
            public DateTime Timestamp { get; set; }
```

Figure 177: POCO

- You need to modify the facets to load only those that are related to succinctlybooks, and not collection1.

- Make sure you use only your fields from your collection.

Finished? Commit your branch if you want!

Summary

In this section, we have learned how we can add a user interface to our Solr search engine. The first option was using the Velocitas response writer, which is built into the downloaded Solr. The second option was using the SolrNets sample application. It's not a finished, full-blown application, but this is an excellent start for something that might make you some money—or save you some money.

Final Words

And with this, we have concluded this e-book, part of the amazing *Succinctly* series from Syncfusion. Let's just take a few minutes to do a final review.

You have an idea or a need. This idea might make you some money or save you some money. Search is an important piece of many of the ideas out there. If you don't do it right, you might frustrate your users, but if you do it properly, you can entice them.

Search used to be difficult and expensive—it used to be a long steep road—but this has all changed. Now, Solr comes to the rescue.

To get your idea up and running, you first have to understand where your data is. There could be multiple data sources, like databases, custom management systems, files, feeds, web pages, or even data entered by your users. There are different ways of getting the data, for example, with crawlers or connectors.

Get to know your data, get your Solr ready, model your data in the schema.xml, configure your Solr in the Solrconfig.xml, and then index your data.

Once you've stored, sorted, and indexed things, your data is searchable via REST.

If you want to take it a step further, you have SolrNet (or SolrJ, Solritas) to help you. You can look at the Solr sample application if you want an easy way to get started. There are other packages and applications that can be used, but I didn't mention them here.

If you've come this far, you are on the right path to do some amazing things with your implementation of Solr in your application.

I am Xavier Morera, and I thank you for staying with me. I hope you've enjoyed reading Solr Succinctly and following along as much as I have enjoyed writing it.

Ping me on Twitter @xmorera if you have questions or comments, or if there is anything I can do to help you.

This is not the end—it is the beginning of your great journey in search!